Microsoft Works on the IBM PC

Phyllis Yasuda and Vivian Frederick
with
Judy Yamada and Ann Koda

Mitchell Publishing, Inc.
Innovators in Computer Education
915 River Street • Santa Cruz, California 95060
(800) 435-2665 • In California (408) 425-3851
A Random House Company

Cover Design: Juan Vargas
Printer: Malloy Lithographing, Inc.
Product Development: Raleigh S. Wilson
Product Management: BMR, of Mill Valley, California
Sponsoring Editor: Roger L. Howell
Text Design: John Richards & Jane Granoff

Printed in the United States of America.
10 9 8 7 6 5 4 3 2

Library of Congress Card Catalog No.: 88-062418

ISBN: 0-394-39547-6 (text only)
        0-394-39544-1 (text and data disk)

Table Of Contents

Appendices:

Preface and Acknowledgements

Microsoft Works on the IBM PC is designed to introduce *Microsoft Works* to students of varying backgrounds, but it is particularly geared toward the computer novice. Throughout this text, our assumption is that the student has little experience with the IBM PC and has never used *Microsoft Works* before; therefore, our approach is comprehensive and gently encouraging. This book consists of a series of worksheet exercises that build gradually on themselves. It is essential that the student read the section, "How to Use This Book," before beginning to work with the individual chapters.

Note that a data disk is packaged with this book (see the inside back cover). This disk contains practice files that are needed to complete the exercises.

Throughout the exercises in the text, reproductions of screen images guide the student every step of the way. These reproductions match the students' own screens as they work through the program. This book covers version 1.05 of *Microsoft Works*.

An instructor's guide is available to accompany this book. The guide provides an annotated copy of the text and contains suggestions for using the book, numerous tips for teaching the material, and a list of pitfalls to be avoided.

A glossary appears at the end of the text; it contains words that are introduced in the book, along with common computer-related terms that the student may be curious about.

We deeply appreciate the support and help of our families throughout the development of this book. We also want to thank the classroom instructors at De Anza College, who have used our exercises for the past four years to teach computing concepts to more than 2,000 students. Suggestions from all of them—particularly Rod Riggenbach, Eric Nagler, Barbara Buckley, and Peggy Miller—have been incorporated into the final version of this book. And we give special thanks to Doris Tengan for sharing her experiences in operating an ice cream shop.

— P.Y., V.F., J.Y., & A.K.

How to Use This Book

Microsoft Works is a powerful, integrated productivity tool that includes word processing, database, spreadsheet, and communications functions. As a user, you can work with any one or all of these functions as you need them. *Microsoft Works on the IBM PC* has been written for the beginning user of the *Microsoft Works* (version 1.05) program. If you are a novice computer user—as well as a new user of *Microsoft Works*—this book will gently guide you through your first encounter with a computer.

Although you may be an expert user of many other software packages, learning a new application presents new challenges and requires a considerable investment of your time. For the experienced user, this book is intended to reduce the amount of time you need to achieve meaningful results with *Microsoft Works* and your IBM personal computer. You will probably skip many of the step-by-step tutorials, but the detailed information in these exercises will be there when you need them.

Microsoft Works on the IBM PC consists of fifteen chapters and eight appendices. Each chapter consists of a worksheet that leads you through the creation or alteration of one or more documents using *Microsoft Works*. The worksheets are presented in the form of keystroke tutorials, in which we list all keyboard entries needed to achieve the stated purpose and then describe the results. Each chapter includes many screen illustrations to supplement the instructions in the text.

Chapter 1 is an introduction to the program, *Microsoft Works*. Chapters 2 through 5 cover word processing features. Chapters 6 through 9 focus on spreadsheet capabilities of the program. Chapters 10 through 13 concentrate on database applications, including report generation. In Chapter 14, you will integrate the major applications; Chapter 15 covers communications capabilities.

The eight appendices address some specific needs of individual users. Appendix A is a short introduction to the IBM computer and keyboard for those who have never used one. Appendix B features recommended procedures for using and protecting your computer system and equipment. Appendix C covers use of the MS/DOS operating system to achieve specific file management and disk management objectives. Appendix D is a guide to installing *Microsoft Works* on your hard disk. Appendix E gives detailed instructions for using *Works* if your system includes two floppy disk drives. Appendix F covers the use of CompuServe. Appendix G contains a number of reference sheets for each of the *Works* modules. Appendix H provides a glossary of frequently used computer terms.

In the following chapters, we assume that your hardware configuration consists of an IBM-XT computer with 640K memory, a monochrome or a color monitor, an internal 20 MB hard disk, one floppy drive, and a dot-matrix printer. Chapter 9 assumes that you have a Hercules-compatible graphics card. Chapter 15 assumes that you have a Hayes-compatible 300 or 1200 baud modem installed in your system. If your computer is equipped with a mouse, you can make menu selections using the mouse instead of the keyboard.

This text also assumes that you are familiar with your IBM computer system, including the use of DOS for some limited file and disk management chores, and that you have followed the instructions in the *Works* manual to install *Works* on your hard disk in a separate *Works* directory. If these assumptions are *not* correct, you should refer to the appropriate appendix for further information.

Tips for Using the Worksheets

We have developed the worksheets in an easy-to-follow format, as shown below:

- Names of files are in italics: *Filename.*
- Menu titles and options are in all caps: FILE.
- The first time a term is used, it will appear in ***italicized boldface***.
- Section headings are designed to help you quickly locate the information you need.
- When you are to take action, the instructions are preceded by an arrow in the left margin, indented, and typed in **bold**.

We have also used many screen illustrations throughout the text to show you *approximately* what your screen should look like as you work through the material. However, due to minor differences in hardware and software, your screen may not look *exactly* like the one in the book. As long as the basic information is there, you are doing fine, but do ask questions when you're uncertain.

Read ahead! Read the section before you actually begin to follow its instructions. Experience has shown that students who read only as they go along miss the action taking place on the screen—and with any computer, that's half the fun! Reading computer screens is also the best way to learn to use any computer program.

Take your time as you work through the exercises, and review the material often. The original document will usually appear on your data disk so that you can start over again whenever you wish.

Feel free to experiment. This book was designed to help you explore some of the operations of *Microsoft Works*. And before you even begin the chapter worksheets, make a backup copy of the data disk that accompanies this book. Then, if you should damage the data disk, you can easily make a new copy and start over again. After you have completed a chapter, see if you can, on your own, get *Works* to do what *you* want it to do. Remember, you needn't worry about making mistakes. In fact, we've found that people learn more from making mistakes, trying to figure out what went wrong, and then making the necessary corrections. So don't hesitate to jump right in!

If you get stuck, try one or more of these methods:

- Browse through the available options. Experienced users often learn a new application program this way.
- Check the "quick reference" sections in the text for each *Works* tool.
- Use the HELP facility.
- Ask your classroom neighbor, instructor, or lab assistant.
- Read the manufacturer's manual *Microsoft Works Reference*, which accompanied the program itself. We recommend it as a source for all kinds of useful facts. (*Note:* The goal of this book is to teach you enough to get started with *Works*; it is *not* designed to replace the *Works* manual.)

1 Introducing
Microsoft Works

Meeting *Works*

Microsoft Works is an integrated software package for professionals and small businesses. The program combines a word processor, a database manager, a spreadsheet, and a telecommunications module. It also includes capabilities for mail merging, report generation, and simple chart generation. None of the separate pieces are as powerful as other individual programs, but all of them together simplify and speed up the tasks of creating and maintaining small databases; preparing and managing spreadsheets; writing memos, letters, and reports; and using dial-up information services.

Setting the Scene

You are the manager of a small ice cream shop, "The Ice Cream Factory." Your boss, Chris Hughes, also owns seven other small ice cream shops, and she has purchased an IBM XT equipped with one floppy disk drive and one 20-megabyte hard disk drive, together with the necessary printer, monitor, and keyboard for each of her shops. In addition to the hardware, she has just taken delivery of eight copies of *Microsoft Works*. She would like you and the other seven managers to use *Microsoft Works* to maintain all the records needed to manage your shops effectively.

Your first assignment is to learn something about the software. The worksheet that follows is designed to help you do that. In order to complete this worksheet, you will need to use the data disk that accompanies this text.

In this worksheet, you will learn how to:

- Insert and remove floppy disks
- Open and close documents
- Use *Works* dialog boxes and menus
- Use your printer

Some Points to Remember

The (SHIFT), (CTRL), and (ALT) keys are programmed to be held down while another key is pressed. As you probably know, when you type a capital letter, you hold down the (SHIFT) while pressing a letter. When you see keys connected by hyphens in this text, you are to hold down the first key(s) while pressing the last key. For example, when you see (CTRL)-(ALT)-(DEL), hold down the (CTRL) and (ALT) keys while you press the (DEL) key.

Getting Started

The correct method for starting the IBM PC depends on the state of the computer.

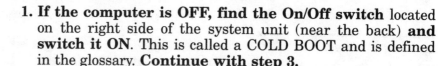

1. **If the computer is OFF, find the On/Off switch** located on the right side of the system unit (near the back) **and switch it ON**. This is called a COLD BOOT and is defined in the glossary. **Continue with step 3.**

2. **If the computer is ON and there is another student's information on the screen, press** (CTRL)-(ALT)-(DEL). (Hold down the (CTRL) and (ALT) keys with your left hand, and keep holding them down while you press the (DEL) key. Release all three keys.) This is called a WARM BOOT and will restart the computer. **Continue with step 3.**

3. **WAIT** while the computer does a self-check of the system. After a few seconds, the red light on Drive C will light up indicating that software is being transferred into memory from the fixed disk.

4. If a request for the current date appears, **type the date** using numbers (for example, 5/1/89 for May 1, 1989), so the computer can date-stamp any files you may create during the current session. **Press** (ENTER) **after typing the date.** If you wish, you may ignore this step by pressing (ENTER).

5. A request for the current time may appear next. **Enter the time** using the 24-hour "military" clock (for example, 13:30 for 1:30 P.M.). **Press** (ENTER) **after typing the time.** Again, you may simply press (ENTER) to bypass this step. You will now see the **C>**.

6. **Follow the instructions on installing** *Microsoft Works* **on your hard disk** (if you have not already done so).

Starting *Works*

1. Type: **cd\works**

2. Press: (ENTER)

3. Type: **works**

4. Press: (ENTER)

The NEW dialog box shown in Figure 1–1 appears with the Word Processor tool selected and <New> highlighted. (Dim the

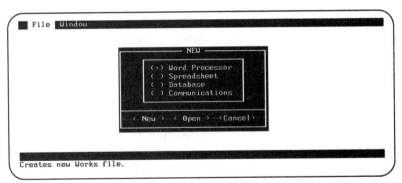

```
■ File  Window

                    ┌─────── NEW ───────┐
                    │ (·) Word Processor │
                    │ ( ) Spreadsheet    │
                    │ ( ) Database       │
                    │ ( ) Communications │
                    │                    │
                    │ ‹ New ›  ‹ Open ›  ‹Cancel› │
                    └────────────────────┘

Creates new Works file.
```

Figure 1-1

Figure 1-2

screen if you cannot see the <> highlighted.) *Note:* If the screen does not appear (for example, a message that the wrong file name was used may appear), **Press** (ENTER) again.

5. Hold the data disk with your thumb on the label and remove the disk from its protective envelope. See Figure 1–2. Do not touch any of the exposed plastic surfaces.

6. Insert the data disk into Drive A with the label up and the exposed plastic oval window entering the drive first. Close the drive door.

Dialog Boxes

Dialog boxes (such as the NEW dialog box shown in Figure 1–1) allow you to communicate with *Works*. Each dialog box contains one or more sections. The (TAB) key and **arrow** keys are used to move the cursor within the box. With a few exceptions, the (TAB) key is used to move from one section to another, and the (↓) and (↑) keys are used to move up and down inside each section. As you move the cursor to different options within a dialog box, the option will be marked. The (ENTER) key is used to inform *Works* that the marked options are to be accepted. *Do not use any of these keys yet.* Instructions for making selections from the NEW dialog box will be given as needed.

More Scene Setting

Here's a specific example for you: Your ice cream shop has just opened in a new neighborhood. You want to create a flyer to distribute in the area to let everyone know that you have arrived. Your boss, Chris, has created a rough draft of such a flyer, but you need to make some changes in it. This rough draft is stored on your data disk under the file name, *Announce.*

Some Points to Remember

A *file* is another name for a document that is electronically stored on a disk and can be easily retrieved for processing by a computer. Each individual document, or file, must have a unique name. The file can be a letter, a list of names, or a program. The IBM PC environment imposes some restrictions on the way file names are formed, but you don't have to worry about that in order to use these worksheets.

Opening a file means to make the file ready for use by bringing it into the computer's main memory from where it is stored on the disk. When you open a file, it's as if you went to a file cabinet, removed the desired document from a folder, and put the document on your desk.

Closing a file means to put the file away. When you close a file, it's as if you put the document in a folder and then closed the folder, leaving it on your desk. Any changes you made in the file will be lost unless you save the file.

Saving a file means to copy the current contents of the file back into its storage place on the disk. When you save a file, it's as if you put a copy of the file back into the folder in the file cabinet. The file remains open, and you can continue to work with the document.

Opening the File

The data disk should be in Drive A; the door of Drive A must be closed; and the NEW dialog box should be showing on the screen.

1. Press: (TAB) **twice** to move the cursor to <Open>.

2. Press: (ENTER) to accept the options marked on the screen. An OPEN dialog box similar to Figure 1–3 will appear. (*Note:* Drive C in your computer may contain some files.)

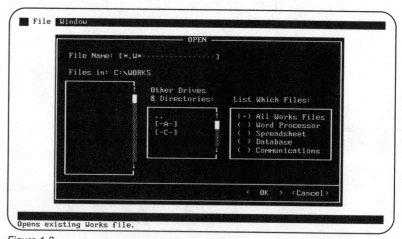

Figure 1-3

3. **The line above the left box should say "Files in: C:\WORKS". If it does, follow steps 3a through 3c below. If it says "Files in A:", go directly to step 4.**

   a. Press the (TAB) key until the cursor is in the center box marked "Other Drives & Directories".

   b. Press the ⓓ key until [-A-] is highlighted.

   c. Press the (ENTER) key to select Drive A.

4. Press: (TAB) until the cursor is in the box titled "List Which Files:".

5. Press: ⓓ to select Word Processor.

6. Press: (ENTER) to list the word processing files in the box on the left.

Think About It

Look at the screen. "A" represents Drive A. You requested the computer to list all word processing files on Drive A. (Your data disk is in Drive A.) The names of word processing files in *Works* end with "WPS" after the period. You should see four file names.

7. Press: (TAB) to move the cursor to the left box.

8. Press: ⓤ or ⓓ to highlight *ANNOUNCE.WPS* (The entire file name should appear on a dark background.)

9. Press: (ENTER) to open the *Announce* file. Your screen should look something like Figure 1–4.

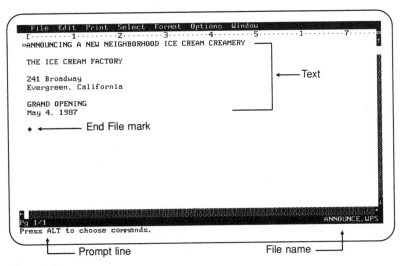

Figure 1-4

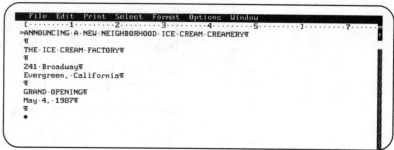

File Edit Print Select Format Options Window
[·······1·······2·······3·······4·······5······]·······7·····
»ANNOUNCING·A·NEW·NEIGHBORHOOD·ICE·CREAM·CREAMERY¶
¶
THE·ICE·CREAM·FACTORY¶
¶
241·Broadway¶
Evergreen,·California¶
¶
GRAND·OPENING¶
May·4,·1987¶
¶
♦

Figure 1-5

Sometimes special characters will appear on your screen (see Figure 1–5).

The displayed symbols indicate the beginning of new lines, tabs, and spaces between characters on word processing files. Locating these special characters may be very helpful later if you have formatting problems.

10. **If your screen displays the special characters, follow steps 10a through 10c to eliminate them from the screen; if not, proceed with the next section on inserting text.**

   a. Press: (ALT) to enter the Menu bar.

   b. Type: **o** (the letter **o**). The OPTIONS menu box will drop showing the options.

   c. Type: **a** (SHOW ALL CHARACTERS option). This will deselect that option and the special characters will not show on screen.

The special characters have been removed from the screen. If you want special characters to be displayed, follow the same procedure; the SHOW ALL CHARACTERS option will be re-selected and special characters will appear.

Inserting Text

Take a minute to look at the screen. The top bar contains menu options. The ruler line marks the screen in inches. The *cursor* (a flashing underscore) should be flashing under the "A" in "Announcing." The ">>" marks the beginning of the file. The "♦" marks the end of the file. The information bars at the bottom of the screen show that you are on page one of a one-page document, and the file you are currently using is titled *AN-NOUNCE.WPS*. The prompt line at the bottom of the screen contains hints about what you can do next. The prompt line will change as you make different selections from the menus.

Work through the following instructions to add the hours of your grand opening:

1. Press: ⓙ **until the cursor** is on the blank line after the date.

2. Press: (CAPS LOCK) **several times** while you look at the bottom right corner of the screen. Note that the letters "CL" alternately appear and disappear as you press the (CAPS LOCK) key to remind you when the key is on. **Leave the** (CAPS LOCK) **key on** while you continue to step 3.

3. Use the numbers at the top of the keyboard to type: **1:00 PM to 4:00 PM** (*Note:* Any zero should have a line through it when displayed on the screen, designating that it is a number and not the letter "O." It is important to use zero for the number "0" and the number one instead of the letter "1." You will also have to remember to use the shift key to obtain the colon. The (CAPS LOCK) *only* works with the alphabet.)

4. Press: (ENTER) to add a blank line under the time.

In the next section of this worksheet you will make some changes to the announcement by choosing selections from the Menu bar at the top of the screen.

Using the Menu Bar

The Menu Bar across the top of the screen should look something like Figure 1–6.

```
 File  Edit  Print  Select  Format  Options  Window
```

Figure 1-6

1. Press: (ALT) to enter the Menu bar. At the top of the screen, one letter of each word will be highlighted and the word "FILE" will appear in reverse video. Gently turn the contrast knob on your screen until the "F" in "FILE" appears different from the rest of the word. It should look something like the copy in Figure 1–7.

```
 File  Edit  Print  Select  Format  Options  Window
```

Figure 1-7

2. Press: (ENTER) and the FILE menu will drop down.

3. Press: → **six times slowly** to view the various menus.

4. Press: ⬅ to return to the FILE menu.

5. Press: (ESC) to return to the document.

Making a Menu Selection

In this section you will use the EDIT menu to delete the blank line immediately above the address line. (See Figure 1–8.)

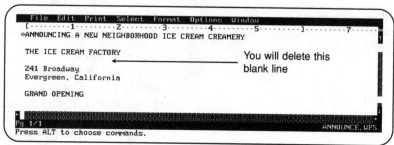

You will delete this blank line

Figure 1-8

Deleting

1. Press: ↑ **until the cursor** is on the blank line between the word "THE" and the number "241".

2. Press: (ALT) to enter the Menu bar.

3. Type: **e** (to select the EDIT menu). The menu box shown in Figure 1–9 with the various edit options will drop.

4. Type: **d** (this selects DELETE).

5. The blank line will disappear. (Aren't computers great for modifying documents?)

Figure 1-9

One more change! The announcement might look better if all the copy were centered. To do this, the complete document must first be highlighted to show that it is selected; then the CENTER option must be chosen from the FORMAT menu.

Selecting and Centering Text

1. Press: ↑ **several times** until the cursor is at the beginning of the file, resting under the "A" in "ANNOUNCING".

2. Press: (F8) **several times** until all of the text lines are highlighted.

3. Press: (ALT) to enter the Menu bar.

4. Type: **t** (this selects the FORMAT menu). The menu box with its options will drop.

5. Type: **c** (this selects the CENTER option). The text will move to the center of the screen.

6. Press: ⓔ to deselect the lines.

As you can see, the appearance of the text is much improved. Now let's turn to the next section to save your file and complete the session.

Saving a File under a Different Name

At the present time, your revision exists only on the screen and in the memory of your computer. If the power should go off, you would have to start over with the original version of *Announce*. Most programs do not automatically save your file as you are creating it.

When you have completed the following steps, your revision of *Announce* will be saved with the file name, *Announ2*, so that the original file will remain unchanged on your disk.

The FILE Menu

Figure 1-10

1. Press: (ALT) to enter the Menu bar. Since **FILE** is already highlighted,

2. Press: (ENTER) The FILE menu box shown in Figure 1–10 will appear.

3. Type: **a** (SAVE AS option). The SAVE AS dialog box similar to Figure 1–11 will appear.

4. Check to see if the Current Drive listed is A. If not, follow steps a, b, and c.

  a. Press: (TAB) until the highlight reaches the Other Drives & Directories box.

  b. Press: ⓙ until [-A-] is highlighted.

  c. Press: (ENTER) You will now see that your current drive option shows that you are in Drive A.

5. Type: **Announ2** The old name will disappear and the new name will replace it.

Figure 1-11

6. Press: (ENTER)   The red light on Drive A will come on and will stay on until the save operation is completed.

Printing a File

The following instructions include all the steps you must take at the computer to print your announcement.

▐▐▐▶ 1. Turn on your printer and check that it is ready to print.

2. Press: (ALT) to enter the Menu bar.

3. Type: **p** (the PRINT menu box will drop).   (See Figure 1–12.)

4. Press: (ENTER) since PRINT is already highlighted. The PRINT dialog box appears. (See Figure 1–13.)

5. Press: (ENTER) to accept the highlighted *default setting* of one copy. Printing will being shortly.

Defaults are suggested settings by the program. You can accept the default settings or change them.

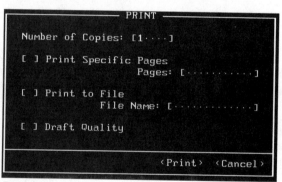

Figure 1-12

Figure 1-13

Quitting *Works*

Now that you have printed your announcement and saved your revised version on the floppy disk, you can quit *Works* and return to it later. Remember that when you quit *Works*, the current file in the computer's memory disappears but any files stored on the disk (either floppy or hard) are not lost.

When you finish using a program, it is always best to formally quit the program. If you do not follow that procedure, information may be lost because the computer updates the directories on the disks during the quitting process. The following instructions will guide you through the steps for quitting *Works*.

▐▐▐▶ 1. Press: (ALT) to enter the Menu bar.

2. Press: (ENTER) since FILE is already highlighted.

3. Type: **x** (to exit the program).

4. **Take your disk out of Drive A and place it in the protective envelope.**

5. **Turn off the computer.**

Congratulations! You should now be able to open and close *Works* files, use menus and dialog boxes, and print documents.

2 Word Processing: Worksheet 1

Introduction

Word processing is perhaps the easiest computer application for laypeople to understand—as well as the most useful. A word processing program is indispensable to many of us because of the computer's ability to save our keystrokes in memory, thus allowing us to easily make any changes we wish before printing our final copy. When relieved of the burden of correcting typographical mistakes, we are able to concentrate on the purpose of writing—to communicate ideas. Revisions are no longer chores but opportunities to improve.

It is well known that computer hardware and word processing software can be used to store documents and recall them at later dates for reuse or revision; to print documents using various typefaces, styles, and sizes; to provide formats with headers and footers; and to print personalized form letters. More recently, some word processors include additional features, which allow them to print in columns and to incorporate graphics into text.

Another extremely useful feature of word processing programs is the manner in which they facilitate collaborative writing. This book was produced by four different authors, all using the same word processing program. A series of disks were exchanged and we edited and revised each other's work until none of us had any sense of ownership of any individual part of the manuscript. This ability to collaborate means that each individual can bring his or her major strengths to bear on the entire project.

Therefore, we think it is natural then that the first part of *Works* which you will use is the word processing tool. You were introduced to this portion of the package in Chapter 1. You should recall that the position at which the action takes place on the screen is marked by a ***cursor***, which in *Works* is a blinking underline character. Also note that, as in most word-processing programs, you should not type a carrier return at the end of a line of typing. The program will "***wordwrap***" and automatically begin a new line when it is needed. Don't forget to press the (ENTER) key, however, whenever a new line would always be required, for example, at a new paragraph or a new item in a list.

1. Use the **arrow** keys to move around the screen. Note that using the arrow keys does not change the layout. (ENTER) will add lines, (BACKSPACE) will erase characters, and (TAB) will move the existing text to the right.

2. To erase a letter, place the cursor under that letter and press (DEL).

3. Press the (ENTER) key at points where a new line would always be required, for example, at a new paragraph.

4. To reverse the last action taken, try selecting UNDO from the EDIT menu.

5. To abandon the present action and return to the previous step, try the (ESC) key; it often works.

6. The (SHIFT), (CTRL), and (ALT) keys are programmed to be held down while another key is pressed. As you probably know, when you type a capital letter, you hold down the (SHIFT) while pressing a letter. When you see keys connected by hyphens in these worksheets, you are to hold down the first key(s) while pressing the last key. For example, when you see (SHIFT)-(→), hold down the (SHIFT) while you press the (→).

Setting the Scene

Imagine the following: You are the manager of "The Ice Cream Factory" and have been given a computer and *Works* to use to better organize the store. Before tackling a major project, you have decided to compose an article on ice cream trivia for the local newspaper. You began the article earlier, but it needs revision.

This worksheet will give you the opportunity to:

- Boot the computer with the *Works* program
- Open a file
- Move the cursor around the text
- Insert, delete, and replace text
- Center, underline, and bold text
- Create paragraphs
- Search and replace text
- Save changes using a new name
- Use the FILE, EDIT, SELECT, FORMAT, and WINDOW menus

Starting *Works*

1. **Follow the instructions for installing *Microsoft Works* onto your hard disk if you have not already done so.**

2. Type: **cd\works** to change the Current Directory to the *Works* directory.

3. Press: (ENTER)

4. Type: **works**

5. Press: (ENTER)

Figure 2-1

The NEW dialog box shown in Figure 2–1 appears with the Word Processor tool selected and <New> highlighted. (Dim the screen if you cannot see the <> highlighted.)

6. Hold your data disk with your thumb on the label, and remove the disk from its protective envelope. Do not touch any exposed plastic surfaces.

7. Insert the data disk into Drive A with the label up and the exposed plastic oval window entering the drive first. Close the drive door.

Reminder: **Insert your data disk only when directed to do so**. Remember that the *Microsoft Works* program is stored on the hard disk in Drive C. The computer will look to Drive A initially to see if you want to run a program other than the one on Drive C. Your data disk contains only data; therefore, if the data disk is in Drive A before *Works* is loaded, an error message similar to "Non-system disk in Drive A" will be generated. The same message will appear if you attempt a warm boot with your data disk in Drive A.

Opening a File

A word-processing file with which you can work has already been prepared for you. This file is stored on the data disk under the file name *TRIVIA.WPS*. The name *Trivia* is intended to help you remember the type of data stored in the file, and the extension ".WPS" is the standard *Works* file extension for word-processing files.

1. Press: (TAB) **two times** to move the cursor selection to <OPEN>.

2. Press: (ENTER)   The OPEN dialog box will appear. See Figure 2–2.

3. Press: (TAB) until the cursor moves to the middle box.

4. Press: (↓) until the [-A-] becomes highlighted.

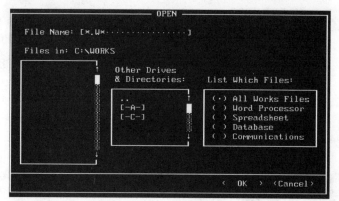

Figure 2-2

5. Press: (ENTER) A list of file names from your data disk in Drive A will appear in the left-hand box.

6. Press: (TAB) **three times.** The cursor will move to the right-hand box.

7. Press: (↓) **one time.** The cursor will move to the word processor line.

8. Press: (ENTER) Your screen should look something like Figure 2–3.

9. Press: (TAB) **one time** to move the cursor to the left-hand box.

10. Press: (↓) until the file name *TRIVIA.WPS* is highlighted.

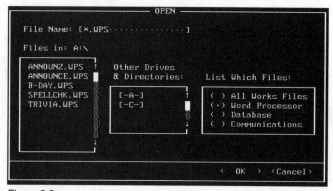

Figure 2-3

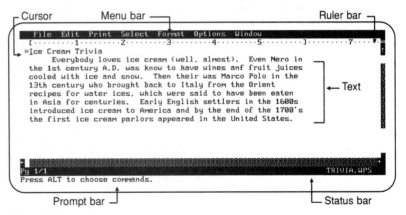

Figure 2-4

11. Press: (ENTER) The *Trivia* file similar to Figure 2–4 will appear on the screen.

As you go through this chapter, you will be directed to make corrections in the *Trivia* document. These corrections are shown by number in Figure 2–5.

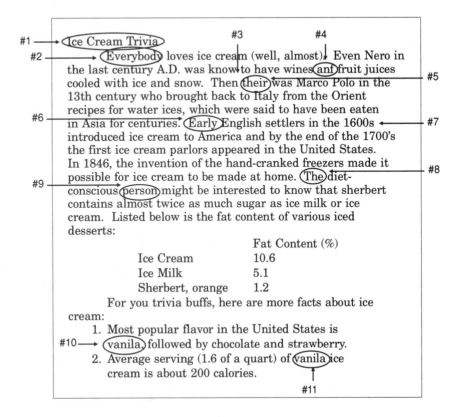

Scrolling around the Text

In order to make corrections easily, you must be able to move the cursor around in the text. Practice moving the cursor (the blinking underline under the first letter in the file) using all the keys and key combinations given in the following list:

1. Press: ⬆ ⬇ ➡ ⬅ to move one character at a time in the direction of the arrows.

2. Press: (PGDN) to move down one screen at a time.

3. Press: (PGUP) to move up one screen at a time.

4. Press: (HOME) to move to the beginning of the line on which the cursor rests.

5. Press: (END) to get to the end of the line on which the cursor rests.

6. Press: (CTRL)-(HOME) (hold down the (CTRL) key, press (HOME), then release both keys) to move to the beginning of the document quickly.

7. Press: (CTRL)-(END) (hold down the (CTRL) key, press (END), then release both keys) to move to the end of the document quickly.

Correction 1: Typing a Centered Bold Heading

The main heading within any document should stand out clearly from the rest of the text. In this section, you will first select and highlight the line with which you want to work; then you will center the line and print it in bold letters.

Figure 2-6

1. **Move the cursor under the first letter in the file** as shown in Figure 2–4. The >> symbol to the left indicates that this is the first line of a page. To select the title for centering,

2. Press: (SHIFT)-➡ (hold down the (SHIFT) key while pressing the ➡) until the entire heading is highlighted.

3. Press: (ALT) to enter the Menu bar at the top of the screen.

4. Type: **t** (the FORMAT menu will drop).

5. Type: **c** (to select the CENTER option). The heading will be centered on the screen.

6. Press: (ALT) to enter the Menu bar.

7. Type: **t** (the FORMAT menu again displays).

8. Type: **b** (selects the BOLD option). The title is now centered and in bold print.

Don't be alarmed if the heading does not appear any "bolder" than it was before. The letter "B" appears in the Status bar at the bottom, indicating that the selected words will be *printed* in bold.

Undoing a Previous Action

Usually you will correct any errors you make by using the (DEL) key. But sometimes you find yourself in a situation where (DEL) does not work. In those instances, try (ESC) to return to the prior step, or select UNDO from the EDIT menu to restore the text to its previous condition.

To see what could happen if you press the wrong key, go through the following steps with the heading still highlighted.

1. Press: (DEL) As you can see, the heading disappeared! But don't panic yet—pressing (DEL) when text is highlighted is a shortcut method of erasing blocks of text.

WARNING: **On an IBM PC, pressing (ENTER) will also delete the highlighted text.** To undo this disaster,

2. Press: (ALT) to enter the Menu bar.

3. Type: **e** to drop the EDIT menu box. Since UNDO is already selected,

4. Press: (ENTER) and the heading magically reappears!

Note: UNDO will reverse the previous action in most instances. Sometimes, however, UNDO does not work. If that happens, try pressing (ALT)-(BACKSPACE) (hold down (ALT) while pressing (BACKSPACE)).

Correction 2: Underlining Text

To emphasize the first word of the article, "Everybody," you will underline it. By now you have probably guessed that changes in the appearance of groups of characters are made through the FORMAT menu. In this case, you will select the material to be underlined by highlighting it; then you will cause it to be underlined.

1. **Move the cursor** to the first letter of the text to be underlined (the letter, "E", in the word "Everybody").

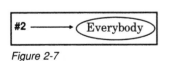

Figure 2-7

2. Press: (SHIFT)-(→) (hold down the (SHIFT) key while pressing (→)) until the text to be underlined is highlighted.

3. Press: (ALT) to enter the Menu bar.

4. Type: **t** (to drop the FORMAT menu box).

5. Type: **u** (to select the UNDERLINE option).

Nothing appears to have changed, but notice that the selected word is illuminated (brighter than the other text) and a **U** appears in the bottom Status bar. The **U** indicates that the word on which the cursor rests will be underlined when printed. When you move the cursor, the word will still be illuminated. Illumination indicates special formatting (bold or underline, for example), but you won't know what that format is until the cursor rests on the selected text and the special formatting feature selected appears in the Status bar.

Corrections 3 and 7: Inserting Text

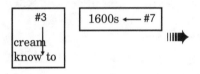

Figure 2-8

Works always inserts letters at the cursor position, simultaneously moving the remaining letters of the line to the right. Therefore, you must always place the cursor at the position where the inserted letter should appear.

1. **Move the cursor to the space between "know" and "to"** in correction 3.

2. Type: **n**

3. **Move the cursor under the *s*** (in *1600s*) in correction 7.

4. Type: **'** (an apostrophe).

Corrections 4 and 5: Replacing Letters

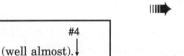

Figure 2-9

There are many ways to replace letters using *Works,* but the easiest way is to use the (DEL) (Delete) key to erase the character or characters at the cursor position and move the text in from the right to fill the deleted space. Next you simply retype the correct text. For example, to correct errors 4 and 5:

1. **Move the cursor under the "f" in "anf".**

2. Press: (DEL) to delete the unwanted letter.

3. Type: **d**

4. **Move the cursor to the "i" in "their".**

5. Press: (DEL) **twice** to delete the unwanted letters.

6. Type: **re**

Corrections 6 and 8: Inserting Paragraphs

The first paragraph in this example is extremely long, so corrections 6 and 8 attempt to divide it into logical paragraphs. In word processing, you must press the (ENTER) key to signal the program that it must always start a new line at that point. *Works* automatically sets default tab stops every five spaces, and you will use the first one for paragraph indentations. To insert a paragraph,

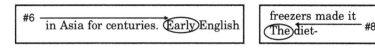

Figure 2-10

⟶ 1. **Move the cursor to the first letter of the new paragraph** (the "E" in "Early" for correction 6).

2. Press: (ENTER) to begin a new line.

3. Press: (TAB) to indent the line five spaces to the right.

4. **Follow the same procedure** to insert the new paragraph in correction 8.

Correction 9: Replacing Words

Figure 2-11

Words can be replaced in the same manner as you used for replacing characters.

⟶ 1. **Move the cursor under the first letter of the word to be replaced—the "p" in "person."** To select the word to be deleted,

2. Press: (SHIFT)-(→) (hold down the (SHIFT) key while pressing the (→)) until the entire word is highlighted.

3. Press: (DEL) to delete the word.

4. Type: **consumer**

Corrections 10 and 11: Searching and Replacing Text

When you noticed that you misspelled the word "vanilla," you were probably concerned that you might have made that same error elsewhere in the document. This is a good example of the use of the search and replace feature, which will search for that misspelled word throughout the file and replace it with the correct spelling. Since the search and replace feature only searches between the present cursor location and the end of the file, you'll first need to move to the beginning of the file.

⟶ 1. Press: (CTRL)-(HOME) (hold down the (CTRL) key, press (HOME)) to move to the beginning of the file.

2. Press: (ALT) to enter the Menu bar.

3. Type: **s** (SELECT menu box drops).

4. Type: **r** to select the REPLACE option. The REPLACE dialog box appears with the cursor in the "Search For:" field.

5. Type: **vanila** which is the misspelled word.

Figure 2-12

6. Press: (TAB) to move to the "Replace With:" field.

7. Type: **vanilla** which is the proper spelling.

8. Press: (TAB) **twice** to the Match Upper/Lower Case field.

9. Press: (↑) to instruct the program to search for both upper and lower case occurrences (an **X** appears in that selection).

To instruct *Works* to stop at every occurrence of "vanila" and display it for your confirmation, you will accept the Replace option. (In actual use, you would probably instruct the program to automatically Search for and Replace all occurrences of misspelled words.) Since it is already highlighted and is the last option you need to set in the dialog box,

10. Press: (ENTER) The first occurrence will appear highlighted, and a dialog box will ask if you would like to replace this occurrence. Since "Yes" is highlighted and you want to accept this option,

11. Press: (ENTER)

12. **Repeat the procedure for any remaining misspelled words.** When all errors are found, the "No more occurrences" dialog box will appear.

13. Press: (ENTER) The dialog box will disappear, and you will have completed making the replacements.

Saving a File under a Different Name

At this point, your revision exists only on the screen and in the memory of the computer. If the power should go off, you would have to start over with the original version of *Trivia*. Remember that most programs do *not* automatically save your file as you are creating it.

In this section, you will save your revision of *Trivia* as *Trivia2* so that the original file will remain unchanged on your disk. As you can imagine, there are times when you will make changes to a document and later decide that the original was better than the revision. Although *Works* has an automatic backup procedure, many programs do not. For that reason, you will save your revision as a new document using a different name.

 1. Press: (ALT) to enter the Menu bar. FILE is already highlighted, so

2. Press: (ENTER)

3. Type: **a** to choose SAVE AS option. When SAVE AS dialog box appears,

4. Type: **Trivia2**   As you type, the old name disappears. The rest of the options need not be changed, so to begin saving,

5. Press: (ENTER)   The red light on Drive A: will be lighted briefly as the file is saved on the disk in that drive.

Viewing Two Open Files

You can assure yourself that you did not destroy the original *Trivia* file, (which still exists in its original form on your floppy disk in Drive A) by opening it again.

1. Press: (ALT) to enter the Menu bar. FILE is selected, so

2. Press: (ENTER)   When the FILE menu box drops,

3. Type: **o** to select **OPEN**.

4. Press: (TAB) until the cursor is in the extreme right-hand box.

5. Press: (↓) to select the Word Processor line.

6. Press: (ENTER)

As you can see, the file you just created, *TRIVIA2.WPS,* is listed in the left box along with the original file, *TRIVIA.WPS.* If you do not see your file, use the (TAB) key to move to the extreme left-hand files box, and keep pressing the (↓). The files box can only show ten files at a time, and since the files are listed alphabetically, you will have to use the (↓) key to view more than ten files. Notice that the program displays all file names in capital letters and adds a three-character *extension* that denotes the tool used to create that file, in this case ".WPS" for the Word Processing tool. To load *Trivia,*

7. Press: (TAB) until the cursor rests in the files list.

8. Press: (↓) until the file you want (*TRIVIA.WPS*) is highlighted.

9. Press: (ENTER)   The *Trivia* file is now displayed. To see that you actually have two files open and resident in memory,

10. Press: (ALT) to enter the Menu bar.

11. Type: **w** to select WINDOW. When the WINDOW menu box drops, you will see two files listed. To return to your revised *Trivia2* file, type the highlighted number preceding the title of the file.

12. If you are not at the beginning of the document, press (CTRL)-(HOME) (Hold down the (CTRL) key and keep it down while you press the (HOME) key. Release both keys.) The cursor will be at the beginning of the file.

Printing a File

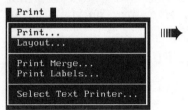

Figure 2-13

In this section, you will print the *Trivia2* file with the corrections you made in it.

1. Turn on your printer and check that it is ready to print.

2. Press: (ALT) to enter the Menu bar.

3. Type: **p** to select the PRINT menu. (See Figure 2–13.)

4. Press: (ENTER) since the PRINT option you need is already selected. The PRINT dialog box appears. (See Figure 2–14.)

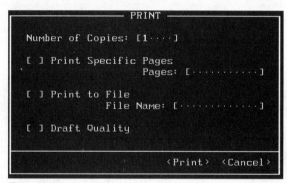

Figure 2-14

5. Press: (ENTER) to accept the highlighted *default setting* of one copy.

Defaults are settings suggested by the program. You can accept the default settings or change them as you wish.

Review

Before completing this section, you should review what you have done earlier. You have opened a file, moved the cursor around the file, inserted and deleted text, centered and made bold the heading, created paragraphs, underlined text, searched and replaced text, and saved a file using a new name. Do you remember which menu was used for each task?

Quitting *Works*

When you finish using a program, it is always best to formally quit the program. If you do not follow that procedure, information may be lost because the computer updates the directories on the disks during the quitting process. The following instructions will guide you through the steps for quitting *Works*.

▶ 1. Press: (ALT) to enter the Menu bar. Since FILE is already highlighted,

2. Press: (ENTER)

3. Type: **x** to exit.

4. Type: **cd** to change the Current Directory to the root (main) directory from which you started.

5. **Take your disk out of Drive A and place it in the protective envelope.**

6. **Turn the computer off.**

3 Word Processing: Worksheet 2

Introduction

When you have completed this chapter, you will **have success-fully**:

- Replaced selected text
- Changed spacing of lines
- Used decimal tabs
- Moved text

Setting the Scene

The article you began correcting in Worksheet 1 now **resembles** Figure 3–1. Areas that still need correction are **marked**.

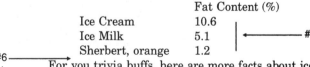

Figure 3-1

Starting *Works*

Figure 3-2

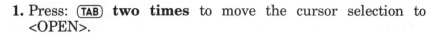

Reminder: **Insert your data disk only when directed to do so.**

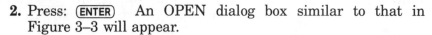

1. Type: **cd\works**
2. Press: (ENTER)
3. Type: **works**
4. Press: (ENTER)

The NEW dialog box appears with the Word Processor tool selected and <New> highlighted as shown in Figure 3–2. (Dim the screen if you cannot see the <> highlighted.)

For this worksheet, you will need to use the file you prepared in Chapter 2. If you followed the directions in that worksheet, the file will be stored on your data disk under the name *TRIVIA2.WPS.*

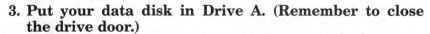

1. Press: (TAB) **two times** to move the cursor selection to <OPEN>.

2. Press: (ENTER)   An OPEN dialog box similar to that in Figure 3–3 will appear.

3. **Put your data disk in Drive A. (Remember to close the drive door.)**

4. Press: (TAB) until the cursor moves to the middle box.

5. Press: ⊕ until [-A-] becomes highlighted.

6. Press: (ENTER)   A list of file names will appear in the left-hand box.

7. Press: (TAB) until the cursor moves to the right-hand box.

8. Press: ⊕ to move the cursor to the Word Processor line.

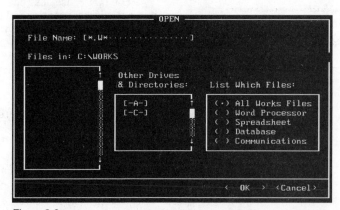

Figure 3-3

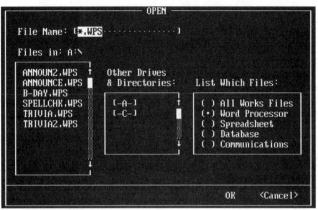

Figure 3-4

9. Press: (ENTER)   Your screen should be similar to Figure 3–4.

10. Press: (TAB) to move the cursor to the left-hand box.

11. Press: (↓) until the file name *TRIVIA2.WPS* is highlighted.

12. Press: (ENTER)   The *Trivia2* file will appear on the screen.

Correction 1: Expanding the Top Margin

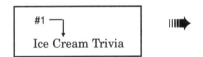

Figure 3-5

The *Works* program automatically assigns one-inch top and bottom margins to word processing documents. To increase the size of the top margin, you will add three lines above the title line.

1. **Place the cursor on the title line.** (It should have appeared there when the file was first loaded. If the cursor is not already at the "I" in "Ice Cream," use (CTRL)-(HOME) to move it there.)

2. Press: (ENTER) **three times** and watch the text move down the screen.

Correction 2: Capitalizing the Title

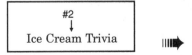

Figure 3-6

Titles are normally in upper-case letters, so to make this correction you will erase the title and retype it using all capital letters. (Some word processing programs have a strikeover mode or allow you to change from upper to lower case without retyping, but *Works* does not include either feature.)

1. Press: (SHIFT)-(→) (hold down (SHIFT) and keep it down while you press (→)) until the entire heading is highlighted. **Release both keys.**

2. Press: (DEL) to delete the title.

3. Press: (CAPS LOCK) until CL appears in the Status bar at the bottom of the screen.

4. Type: **ICE CREAM TRIVIA**

5. Press: (CAPS LOCK) The letters "CL" will disappear from the Status bar.

Correction 3: Typing a Byline

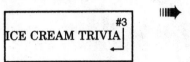

Figure 3-7

You will want to identify yourself as the author of this report. To do so, just follow these steps:

1. Press: (ENTER) **twice** to leave a blank space between your title and byline.

2. Type your name. Since you are still in CENTER mode, your name will be centered.

3. Press: (ENTER) to leave a blank line between your name and the body of the report.

Correction 4: Double Spacing Paragraphs

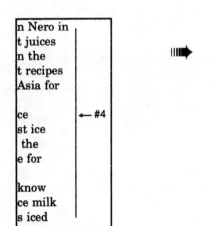

Figure 3-8

Reports are normally typed as double spaced documents (one blank line between each line of typing). The following instructions tell you how to double space the first paragraphs quickly. You will be moving the cursor and highlighting the entire block, then using the menus to choose the double space option.

1. Move the cursor to the left margin of the first line of the first paragraph. (See Figure 3–9.)

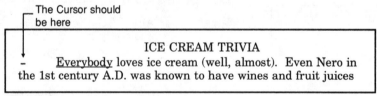

Figure 3-9

2. Press: (SHIFT)-(↓) (hold down (SHIFT) and keep it down while pressing the (↓)) until the first three paragraphs are highlighted. **Release both keys.**

3. Press: (ALT) to enter the Menu bar at the top of the screen.

4. Type: **t** (the FORMAT menu box will drop).

5. Type: **d** to select the DOUBLE SPACE option.

It may look like your report has disappeared, but actually the extra lines introduced by double spacing made the report longer so it occupies more computer screens. To get back to the beginning of the report *and* eliminate the highlighting,

7. Press: (CTRL)-(HOME)

Correction 5:
Correcting a Tab Stop

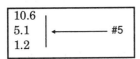

Figure 3-10

To improve the appearance of the table, you need to align the amounts at the decimal point and center the column under the columnar heading, "Fat Content (%)". You can accomplish both of these tasks by eliminating the present tab for the percent column and setting a decimal tab so the column will begin printing about one-half inch further to the right.

Deleting the Existing Tab

1. Press: (PGDN) and (↑) or (↓) until you have the columnar text on screen. The screen should look something like Figure 3–11.

2.

	Fat Content (%)
Ice Cream	10.6
Ice Milk	5.1
Sherbert, orange	1.2

For you trivia buffs, here are more facts about ice cream:
1. Most popular flavor in the United States is vanilla, followed by chocolate and strawberry.
2. Average serving (1/6) of a quart of vanilla ice cream is about 200 calories.

Figure 3-11

Move the cursor to the extreme left margin of the line containing "Ice Cream". (See Figure 3–12.)

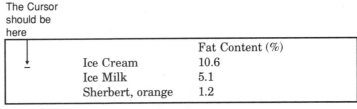

The Cursor should be here

Figure 3-12

3. Press: (SHIFT)-(↓) (hold (SHIFT) down and keep it down while you press (↓)) **three times.** The three lines of the table will become highlighted.

4. Press: (ALT) to enter the Menu bar.

5. Type: **t** to display the FORMAT menu box.

6. Type: **t** to select the TABS option. A dialog box appears as in Figure 3–13.

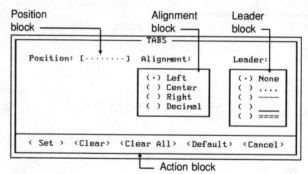

Figure 3-13

There are four information blocks in this dialog box—Position, Alignment, Leader, and Action blocks. In order to move from one block to another, you will use the (TAB) key; to move within a block, you will use the arrow keys. To move between the action items listed along the bottom of the screen, use the (TAB) key.

The cursor currently rests in the Position block.

7. Type: **3.5** (You need to clear this position, which is occupied by the tab.) Since you are erasing a tab, the instructions that follow will cause you to skip the next two blocks.

8. Press: (TAB) **several times** until <Clear> is selected.

9. Press: (ENTER) to complete the procedure. The dialog box will disappear and the numbers will move to the left near the words. That happened because you eliminated the tab that controlled the percent amounts column. In the next section, you are going to set a new tab for that column.

Setting the New Tab

Setting a *decimal tab* causes the decimal points to line up vertically. The process is much the same as setting any tab. Since you are reformatting an existing table, you must first be sure that the table is highlighted. (The table should still be highlighted from the previous exercise.) By following the steps given below, you will set a tab four inches from the left margin so the decimals in the percent amounts align vertically:

1. Press: (ALT) to activate the Menu bar.

2. Type: **t** to select the FORMAT menu.

3. Type: **t** to select the TABS option.

4. Type: **4** to indicate that the tab should be set four inches from the left.

5. Press: (TAB) **once** to move to the Alignment box where you will select the decimal tab.

6. Press: (↓) **three times** until the cursor rests beside the Decimal option. Notice that you could choose to have the column align at the left, center, or right. To leave your selection at Decimal and move to the Leader block,

7. Press: (TAB) You may choose to use periods, hyphens, underscores, or equal signs as leaders. To select periods,

8. Press: (↓) **once**.

9. Press: (TAB) **once** to select the SET option.

10. Press: (ENTER) The dialog box will disappear, and the column of numbers will be neatly aligned below the columnar heading.

Correction 6: Inserting Blank Lines

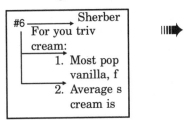

Figure 3-14

Double spacing is necessary: (1) above and below the paragraph which appears under the table, and (2) between the enumerated paragraphs. (See Figure 3–14.)

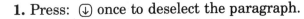

1. Press: (→) once to deselect the table and move the cursor to the beginning of the paragraph under the table.

2. Press: (SHIFT)-(↓) (hold down (SHIFT) and press (↓)) until the two lines are selected.

3. Press: (ALT) to activate the Menu bar at the top of the screen.

4. Type: **t** (the FORMAT menu box drops).

5. Type: **d** to select the DOUBLE SPACING option. The menu disappears, and the paragraph becomes double spaced.

The enumerated paragraphs look good single-spaced, but there should be a blank line between them. To insert the blank line,

1. Press: (↓) once to deselect the paragraph.

2. Press: **arrow** keys until the cursor is under the number 2 marking the second enumerated paragraph. To insert the extra line,

3. Press: (ENTER) Don't worry if the funny little symbol, >>, appears at the left margin. That's the way *Works* marks the beginning of a page for printing.

4. Press: (CTRL)-(END) (hold down (CTRL) and press (END), then release both) to move the cursor to the end of the file.

Look at the Status bar at the bottom of the screen and you'll see that you are now on page 1/1. That means page number 1 of one total pages. If your screen displays 2/2 (page 2 of a two-page document), you simply have extra lines in your text.

Correction 7: Moving a Paragraph

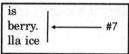

Figure 3-15

Very often you will type a paragraph and decide that it belongs in another part of the document. When that happens, you will want to move the paragraph (sometimes called "cut and paste"). In this exercise you will reverse the order of the enumerated paragraphs at the end.

1. **Move the cursor to the beginning of the second (#2) enumerated paragraph.**

2. Press: (F8) to mark the cursor position as the beginning of a selected block. The word "Extend" will appear in the Status bar.

3. Press: (↓) **twice** to select the paragraph.

4. Press: (ALT) to enter the Menu bar.

5. Type: **e** to select the EDIT menu.

6. Type: **m** to select the MOVE option.

Have you been reading the Status bar and the Prompt bar at the bottom of the screen? **Look at them now.** To select the new location,

7. Press: (↑) until the cursor rests under the number 1.

8. Press: (ENTER) Paragraph 2 now appears before paragraph 1.

Although the paragraphs are now in proper order, they need to be renumbered. If during the move the blank line that you previously inserted disappeared, reinsert it again.

9. **Use the skills you have developed using this worksheet to renumber the paragraphs and add blank lines as desired.**

When you are through, your file should be similar to Figure 3–16.

Saving a File

Since you've made changes in the file, it's important that you save the altered file under a different name so that if you decide the original was better than the revision, you will still have that original copy. Use the skills you developed in Chapter 2 to save your new file under the name *MYTRIVIA.WPS*.

ICE CREAM TRIVIA

Jane Doe

Everybody loves ice cream (well, almost). Even Nero in the 1st century A.D. was known to have wines and fruit juices cooled with ice and snow. Then there was Marco Polo in the 13th century who brought back to Italy from the Orient recipes for water ices, which were said to have been eaten in Asia for centuries.

Early English settlers in the 1600's introduced ice cream to America and by the end of the 1700's the first ice cream parlors appeared in the United States. In 1846, the invention of the hand-cranked freezers made it possible for ice cream to be made at home.

The diet-conscious consumer might be interested to know that sherbert contains almost twice as much sugar as ice milk or ice cream. Listed below is the fat content of various iced desserts:

	Fat Content (%)
Ice Cream	10.6
Ice Milk	5.1
Sherbert, orange	1.2

For you trivia buffs, here are more facts about ice cream:

1. Average serving (1/6 of a quart) of vanila ice cream is about 200 calories.

2. Most popular flavor in the United States is vanilla, followed by chocolate and strawberry.

Figure 3-16

Printing the File without Footers

1. **Turn on your printer and check that it is ready to print.**

2. Press: (ALT) to enter the Menu bar.

3. Type: **p** to select the PRINT menu.

4. Type: L to choose the LAYOUT option.

5. Press: (TAB) until the Footer line is highlighted. Since the page number is not necessary for a one-page document,

6. Press: (DEL) to remove the text in the Footer line.

7. Press: (ENTER) Now you are ready to print.

8. Press: (ALT) to enter the Menu bar.

9. Type: **p** to select the PRINT menu. Since PRINT is already highlighted,

10. Press: (ENTER) and look at the default settings. Since these settings are acceptable,

11. Press: (ENTER) Printing should start in a few seconds.

Review

If time permits, load *Trivia2* again and try to make the corrections without looking at the directions.

Think About It

Congratulations! Your article is now ready to submit. By now you should be able to type text, insert and delete text, change line spacing, set tabs, and move text. If you should be asked to make changes, you can easily recall this file and print a new version with minimum effort.

Quitting *Works*

The following instructions will guide you through the steps for quitting *Works*.

1. Press: (ALT) to enter the Menu bar. Since FILE is already highlighted,

2. Press: (ENTER)

3. Type: **x** to select the EXIT option.

4. Type: **cd**

5. Press: (ENTER)

6. **Take your disk out of Drive A and place it in the protective envelope.**

7. **Turn the computer off.**

4 Word Processing: Worksheet 3

Setting the Scene

As part of your sales promotion activities for The Ice Cream Factory, you originated the idea of sponsoring a "Birthday Club." Birthday Club members will be given a free ice cream cone during the month of their birthday and will be invited to bring a guest. You are now going to create a form letter that can be mailed with the gift certificates each month to the Birthday Club members for that month. You already have created a database containing a list of customers who are members of the Birthday Club.

When you have completed this chapter, you will have successfully:

- Created a file (letter)
- Edited the file using techniques presented in previous pages
- Changed the layout (appearance) of a document
- Saved and printed a new file

Starting *Works*

Reminder: **Do not insert your data disk until directed to do so**.

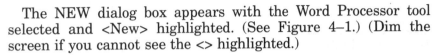

1. Type: **cd\works**

2. Press: (ENTER)

3. Type: **works**

4. Press: (ENTER)

Figure 4-1

The NEW dialog box appears with the Word Processor tool selected and <New> highlighted. (See Figure 4-1.) (Dim the screen if you cannot see the <> highlighted.)

5. Insert your data disk in Drive A.

Opening a New File

For this worksheet, you are going to create your own document from scratch, so there is no file stored on the disk for you to use. You must open a blank word processing document in order to create your Birthday Club letter. Think of this activity as

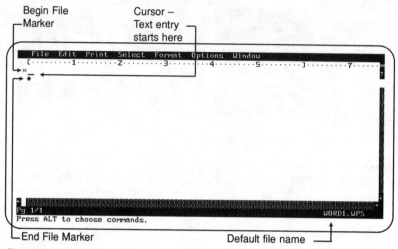

Begin File Marker

Cursor – Text entry starts here

End File Marker

Default file name

Figure 4-2

analogous to reaching into your desk drawer and pulling out a fresh sheet of paper upon which you will start writing.

1. Press: (TAB) **one time.** The cursor will move to <New>.

2. Press: (ENTER)   An almost blank screen will appear. (See Figure 4–2.)

The three symbols clustered together in the upper left corner of the screen are the ***Begin File Marker***, the ***Cursor***, and the ***End File Marker***. As you enter text, it will appear on the screen at the cursor position. The Begin File Marker will, of course, remain where it is. You will not be able to move the cursor backwards over it. The End File Marker will move down as you enter text. You will not be able to move the cursor forward over it.

The file name at the lower right corner of the screen is the ***default*** file name. A default file name is one that *Works* automatically assigns. When you save your Birthday Club letter, you will give it a more descriptive file name. For now, however, you are ready to enter the text of the letter.

Typing the Letter

As you type the letter, it is better to just enter text and not stop to make corrections. After you finish, you can go back and proofread the text you have entered and make any corrections that are needed. Use the (ENTER) key *only* where you want to leave blank lines or start a paragraph.

If you have problems thinking of a letter, you may copy the following letter (see Figure 4–3). We hope you will make changes as you type, however!

December 20, 1987 ———————— Type this line at the top margin

————————————— Press (ENTER) 4 times

Dear Birthday Club Member:

HAPPY BIRTHDAY! ————— Leave 1 blank line here and here

To help you celebrate your special day next month, we are
enclosing 2 coupons that can be exchanged for free ice cream ├— single space
cones in any of our delicious flavors.

————————— 1 blank line here

Our flavor of the month is Banana Pecan, but of course you
may choose from any of our traditional flavors. ├— single space

We are looking forward to seeing you next month! — Blank lines here and here

Yours truly,

————————— Press (ENTER) 5 times

THE ICE CREAM FACTORY
(*Your Name*), Manager ——————— Type your name on this line

Enclosures ┤— Leave 1 blank line
here and here

P.S. Please tell your friends about our Birthday Club.
Just have them drop by our shop and pick up an application
form.

Figure 4-3

Making Changes in Default

Works automatically prints page numbers at the bottom of each page. Since your letter should not be numbered at the bottom, you should first change the *layout* of the file. Layout refers to the appearance of the page as a whole when printed. To see the LAYOUT dialog box,

1. Press: (ALT) to enter the Menu bar.

2. Type: **p** to select the PRINT menu.

3. Type: **L** to select the LAYOUT option. The LAYOUT dialog box will drop, as in Figure 4–4.

This dialog box is used to change margins, the size of the paper to be used for printing, the *header* (a line of text that is automatically printed at the top of each page) and the *footer* (a line of text that is automatically printed at the bottom of each page). The cursor is initially in the first field—"Top Margin".

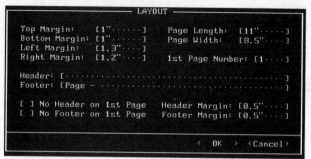

┌─────────────── LAYOUT ───────────────┐

Top Margin: [1"·····]   Page Length: [11"·····]
Bottom Margin: [1"·····]   Page Width: [8.5"····]
Left Margin: [1.3"····]
Right Margin: [1.2"····]   1st Page Number: [1 ····]

Header: [·····································]
Footer: [Page ─ ·····························]

[ ] No Header on 1st Page   Header Margin: [0.5"····]
[ ] No Footer on 1st Page   Footer Margin: [0.5"····]

                              < OK > <Cancel>

Figure 4-4

You will change the default to two and one-half inches and delete the Footer. The other default settings are correct.

1. Type: **2.5**

2. Press: (TAB) until the cursor is in the FOOTER field.

3. Press: (DEL) to delete the page notation. Since all the other settings are correct,

4. Press: (TAB) until the cursor is in the <OK> field.

5. Press: (ENTER) to accept the amended page setup.

Saving a File

1. Press: (ALT) to enter the Menu bar. Since FILE is highlighted,

2. Press: (ENTER)   The FILE menu will drop down.

3. Type: **a** to select the SAVE AS option. The SAVE AS dialog box will appear. Notice that you are in Drive A where your data disk resides.

4. Type: **birthday**   As you type, the old name disappears. The rest of the options need not be changed, so to begin saving,

5. Press: (ENTER)   The red light on Drive A will be lighted briefly, as the file is saved on the disk in that drive.

Printing the File

1. **Turn on your printer and check that it is ready to print.**

2. Press: (ALT) to enter the Menu bar.

3. Type: **p** to select the PRINT menu. Since the option you need, PRINT, is already selected,

4. Press: (ENTER) to obtain the PRINT dialog box. Since all the defaults displayed are acceptable,

5. Press: (ENTER)   Printing should start in a few seconds.

If you need to make any corrections, do so now, then SAVE and PRINT again.

Review

If time permits, create another letter or report with new margins and tabs. Perhaps you'd like to create a letter to your instructor, suggesting improvements for the first portion of this text? Try incorporating the bold, underline, and center options.

Quitting *Works*

The following instructions will guide you through the steps for quitting *Works*.

1. Press: (ALT) to enter the Menu bar. Since FILE is already highlighted,

2. Press: (ENTER)

3. Type: **x** to select the EXIT option.

4. Take your disk out of Drive A and place it in the protective envelope.

5. Turn the computer off.

5 Word Processing Shortcuts and Other Features

Setting the Scene

Now that you are able to produce simple documents, you will want to learn some keyboard shortcuts and learn to "dress up" documents before submitting them to Chris. In this chapter, you will learn to:

- Use keyboard shortcuts to move through a document
- Use keyboard shortcuts to edit, copy, and format text
- Change style and size of typefaces
- Change margins and tabs
- Change layouts
- Insert page breaks

You will notice that the instructions in this chapter are less detailed, leaving more to your imagination. In order to try out these features, you must either create a new report or recall the latest version of *Trivia*. You should feel a real sense of accomplishment when you complete this chapter!

Word Processing Shortcuts

Following are shortcuts for some of the most commonly used functions in word processing. This is not a complete list. Consult the *Microsoft Works Reference* manual for further information.

Selection Shortcuts

The (F8) key enables you to quickly select a block of text or data.

 1. Press: (F8) (the word "Extend" will appear in the Status bar), **then select ONE of the following four options:**

To select	Press these keys
A word	(F8) one more time
A sentence	(F8) two more times

| A paragraph | (F8) three more times |
| An entire file | (F8) four more times |

3. Press: (ESC) to clear "Extend" from Status bar.

4. Press the (→) key to eliminate the highlight.

WARNING: **Do not press** (ENTER) **to eliminate the highlight!** Doing so will erase the entire highlighted area. If you do eliminate the highlighted area accidentally, press (ALT)-(BACKSPACE) to recover the text.

Cursor Movement Shortcuts

To move to	**Press these keys**
Beginning of file	(CTRL)-(HOME)
End of file	(CTRL)-(END)
Right one word	(CTRL)-(→)
Left one word	(CTRL)-(←)

Text Formatting Shortcuts

To change formatting BEFORE typing text, do the following:

To do this	**Press these keys**	**To exit, press**
Bold	(CTRL)-**B**	(CTRL)-[SPACEBAR]
Center	(CTRL)-**C**	(ENTER), then press (CTRL)-**X**
Underline	(CTRL)-**U**	(CTRL)-[SPACEBAR]
Double Space	(CTRL)-**2**	(CTRL)-**1**

To change formatting AFTER text has been typed:

1. Select text.

2. Press necessary keys for desired format, as described earlier.

3. Press: (→) to remove the highlight.

Undo Shortcut

To undo the previous action, press (ALT)-(BACKSPACE)

Type Faces, Styles, and Sizes

The variety of *typefaces*, styles, and sizes are dependent upon your printer's capabilities. *Works* uses the word, "fonts," to refer to the design used to print characters, for example, Courier, Helvetica, or Times. *Works* also has fonts called Pica and Elite.

Typestyles are variations used on fonts (for example, bold, italics, or underline). When choosing the size, the larger the number chosen, the larger the print.

To change the settings, you would do the following:

1. Select the text to be changed.

2. Choose the FORMAT menu.

3. From the FORMAT menu, choose CHARACTER. The TYPEFACE, STYLE, and SIZE options available to you will be displayed.

4. Select the desired option (BOLD, ITALIC, UNDERLINE, STRIKETHROUGH) using the (TAB) key to move to that option, then pressing (←). An X will appear in the selected slot.

5. When all selections are marked, since <OK> is already highlighted, press (ENTER).

You do not have to use the same character setting for the entire document. If you have a dot matrix or laser printer, you will be able to change typeface, typestyle and size within the document. For example, increase the size of your heading to 18 points to see how this feature can improve the appearance of your document.

Changing Margins and Tabs

Margins and tabs are controlled by the LAYOUT dialog box in the PRINT menu and by the TAB dialog box of the FORMAT menu. If none of these have been changed, the following margin defaults (automatic settings) exist in *Works:*

Top Margin:	1 inch
Bottom Margin:	1 inch
Left Margin:	1.3 inches
Right Margin:	1.2 inches
Page Length:	11 inches
Page Width:	8.5 inches

Changing Margins

1. Choose the PRINT menu.

2. Choose the LAYOUT option.

3. Change whatever measurements you want by using the (TAB) key to reach the options and typing over existing defaults.

You may change the settings before or after typing your document.

Changing Tabs

1. Choose the FORMAT menu.

2. Choose the TABS option.

3. Change tabs as desired in the TABS dialog box.

Formatting Paragraphs

When you select PARAGRAPH from the FORMAT menu, the PARAGRAPH dialog box appears. Some items in that dialog box are explained in the following sections.

Alignment

There are four selections which allow you to choose how text is to be aligned:

1. LEFT is the default that causes all text to be printed flush against the left margin.

2. CENTER centers the entire paragraph.

3. RIGHT will line up text against the right margin.

4. JUSTIFIED causes both the left and right margins to be even by adding spaces between words to fill out the line.

Hanging Paragraphs

This feature occurs when the first line of each paragraph is "outdented" rather than "indented"—that is, the first line hangs out farther to the left than the rest of the paragraph does. This accents the first line more and is useful in files such as bibliographies where the last name of an author is outdented or when typing enumerated paragraphs where the numbers stand off to the left.

To understand this feature, you will have to understand a few more of the options from the PARAGRAPH dialog box:

1. LEFT INDENT: This is the left margin. This does not apply to the first line of the paragraph. This determines how far from the left side of the page the body of your paragraph will print.

2. FIRST LINE INDENT: This applies to the first line of a paragraph and is relative to the Left Indent setting.

3. RIGHT INDENT: This is the right margin. This determines how far from the right side of the paper your text will print.

For example, the following steps and settings were used to align the numbered lines above:

⫸ **1.** Select the FORMAT menu.

2. Select the PARAGRAPH option. Type the following settings:
Left Indent: **.5**   First Line Indent: **-.5**

3. Press: (ENTER)

4. Select FORMAT menu again.

5. Select TAB option.

6. Set a tab setting at **.5**.

When typing the enumerated paragraphs, be sure to use the (TAB) key between the number and the first word of the text.

Copying Paragraph Formats

Using the copy format feature simplifies document typing when there are specific paragraph formats (for example, margins, tabs, line spacing) or character formats (for example, bold, underline, italic) that will be used sporadically throughout a document. This process is almost identical to copying and moving text. Try doing the following with a chosen paragraph format:

⫸ **1.** Place the cursor anywhere in the chosen paragraph.

2. Choose the EDIT menu.

3. Select the COPY SPECIAL option. Nothing seems to have happened; however, you will now notice the word "COPY" displayed in the Status bar.

4. Move the cursor to the paragraph you wish to change or to the location where you will be using that same format.

5. Press: (ENTER)   A dialog box will appear. Notice there are two choices.

6. Use the ⓓ to select the PARAGRAPH FORMAT option. Since <OK> is already highlighted,

7. Press: (ENTER)   The paragraph will now conform to the original paragraph format. For example, if the original paragraph had two-inch margins, used single spacing and was printed in italics, the new paragraph would also appear with that format.

Line Spacing

To change the line spacing:

⇒ 1. Choose the FORMAT menu, and select the SINGLE SPACE or DOUBLE SPACE option.

Nesting and Unnesting Paragraphs

Nesting is very useful when formatting quotes within a body of text or when it is desirable to set off a particular paragraph from the rest of the text. To perform this function:

⇒ 1. Select the paragraph or desired text.

2. Press: (CTRL)-N   The left margin of the selected text will move in to the next default tab stop (five spaces).

3. If you do not like this format and would like to reverse it, press (CTRL)-M

Try this feature with any paragraph in your document. If you want to change the right margin by the same amount as the left, use the PARAGRAPH option from the FORMAT menu and increase the right margin by five spaces.

Page Breaks

When typing text in a new file, *Works* automatically inserts a page break according to the page length and margin settings established in LAYOUT. The default is set for 8 1/2" x 11" paper. (You can change the settings through the Print/Layout menu.) If you insert or delete text, *Works* automatically adjusts the page breaks.

On your screen, automatic page breaks are marked with double arrows, **>>**, in the left margin. Manual page breaks are marked with a dotted line. When you insert a manual page break, *Works* automatically readjusts the automatic page breaks that follow it.

To insert a page break:

⇒ 1. Move the cursor to the beginning of the paragraph (or line) where you want to begin a new page.

2. Press: (CTRL)-(ENTER)

To delete a manual page break:

⇒ 1. Select manual page break.

2. Press: (DELETE)

To prevent page breaks within a paragraph:

⇒ 1. Select a paragraph.

2. Choose the FORMAT menu.

3. Select the PARAGRAPH option.

4. Use (TAB) key to move to KEEP PARAGRAPH TOGETHER option.

5. Use (↑) to place an X in that box. Since <OK> is already highlighted,

6. Press: (ENTER)

You have had the opportunity to use many of *Works'* word processing features. To learn more, choose either the HELP INDEX or TUTORIAL INDEX from the WINDOW menu, or refer to the *Microsoft Works Reference* manual.

6 Spreadsheets: Worksheet 1

Introduction to Spreadsheets

In the chapter that follows, you will have the opportunity to work with the *spreadsheet* portion of *Microsoft Works*.

Spreadsheet programs are immensely popular; one in four personal computer owners owns one. VisiCalc™ popularized the concept; two of the most popular spreadsheet programs today are EXCEL™ and Lotus 1-2-3™, which has become the standard by which others are measured. Let's try to discover why so many people from diverse backgrounds find these programs useful for their personal or occupational use.

Spreadsheet programs allow you to automate what you used to do with pencil, paper, and calculator. They create in memory an enormous grid of several thousand horizontal *rows* and hundreds of vertical *columns*—a very small portion of which you will be able to see on screen at any one time. Figure 6–1 shows a typical spreadsheet.

You can scroll through the entire spreadsheet by using the keyboard arrow keys to move the highlight from cell to cell. The block located at the intersection of each row and column is called a *cell.* You can type alphabetic or numeric labels, values, arithmetic or logical instructions, or formulas in the cells. If a

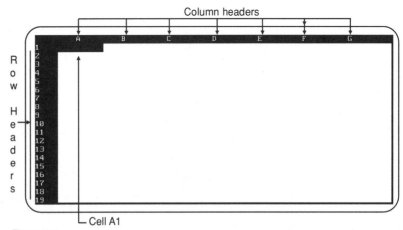

Figure 6-1

cell contains a formula, the spreadsheet will apply that formula to any appropriate value you type into the cell so that as you type data the program performs the calculations you request. If you want to change some numbers, go ahead and change them—the program will automatically recalculate the results of the formulas for you. The formulas can be as simple as addition and subtraction or as complex as trigonometric equations and logical comparisons.

Despite the wide variety of spreadsheet programs available, there is a great deal of similarity between them. As a result, once you learn one, it is relatively easy to adapt to another.

Setting the Scene

Chris Hughes created a spreadsheet on which she plans to itemize sales by category for each day of the week. The spreadsheet contains formulas which will compute Total Sales for the day and add the Taxes Collected to compute the final column, Total Receipts. At the end of each week, the spreadsheet has been programmed to total the sales for each category, compute Total Sales, Taxes Collected, and Total Receipts for the week. Chris has now decided that the spreadsheet needs some modification and asks you if you would make the correction for her. A printout of the spreadsheet appears in Figure 6–2.

In working with the material that follows, you will

- Identify rows, columns, and cells
- Move the highlight around a spreadsheet
- Understand the difference between labels and values
- Enter and delete characters
- Enter and clear cells
- Change cell contents

Combine and change names

```
   File  Edit  Print  Select  Format  Options  Chart  Window
"DAILY RECEIPTS
        A         B         C       D      E       F      G       H       I
1    DAILY RECEIPTS
2    Week of    December 21, 1987
3                                                        Total   Taxes   Total
4       Day    Cone/Cup Fountain Party Pre-pk Hand-pk  Sales   Collect  Rec.
5
6    Sunday       251      123    186    24     51      635     0.21     635
7    Monday       125       67    125    13     32      362     0.24     362
8    Tuesday      164       68     95    18     42      387     0.21     387
9    Wednesday    159       73    152    38     39      461     0.18     461
10   Thursday     186       86    152    21     35      480     0.12     480
11   Friday       248      106    168    17     57      596     0.36     596
12   Saturday     287      157    211    32     65      752     0.45     752
13
14   TOTALS     1,420      680  1,089   163    321    3,673     1.77   3,675
15         ===================================================================
16
17
18
19
                                                              RECEIPTS.WKS
A1
Press ALT to choose commands.
```

Figure 6-2

- Observe the difference between cell content and cell display
- View formulas and functions

Starting *Works*

Figure 6-3

1. Follow the instructions for installing *MicroSoft Works* to your hard disk if you have not already done so.

2. Type: **cd\works** to change the Current Directory to the *Works* directory.

3. Press: (ENTER)

4. Type: **works**

5. Press: (ENTER)

The NEW dialog box appears with the Word Processor tool selected and <New> highlighted. (See Figure 6–3.) (Dim the screen if you cannot see the <> highlighted.)

Opening a File

A Spreadsheet file named *RECEIPTS.WKS* has already been prepared for you and is stored on your data disk. The name *Receipts* is intended to help you remember the type of data stored in the file, and the extension ".WKS" is the standard *Works* file extension for spreadsheet files. Since you want to open an existing file, not start a New file,

1. Press: (TAB) until <OPEN> is highlighted.

2. Press: (ENTER)   The OPEN dialog box will appear as shown in Figure 6–4.

3. Press: (TAB) until the cursor moves to the middle box.

4. Press: (↓) until the [-A-] option is highlighted.

5. Insert your data disk in Drive A.

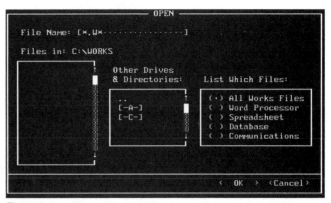

Figure 6-4

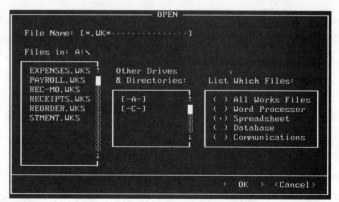

Figure 6-5

6. Press: (ENTER)   A list of file names will appear in the left-hand box.

7. Press: (TAB) to move the cursor to the right-hand box.

8. Press: (↓) to move cursor to the Spreadsheet option.

9. Press: (ENTER)

Your screen should look somewhat like Figure 6–5.

10. Press: (TAB) to move the cursor to the left-hand box.

11. Press: (↓) until the file name *RECEIPTS.WKS* is highlighted.

12. Press: (ENTER)   The *Receipts* file shown in Figure 6–6 will appear on the screen.

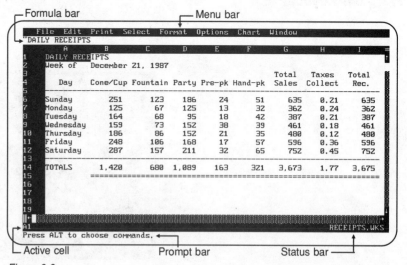

Figure 6-6

Identifying Rows, Columns, and Cells

Notice that the menu items are essentially the same as those in word processing, but the screen itself is labelled across the top by letters and down the left side by numbers. The letters label vertical *columns* and the numbers label the horizontal *rows*. A column and row intersect to form a *cell.* To refer to a cell, you use the cell *address* or location which includes the letter of the column and the number of the row in which the cell is located. For example, the sales of cones and cups on Sunday is located in Cell B6 (Column B, Row 6). Can you name the cell that contains fountain sales for Wednesday? (Answer: C9)

Probably the first thing you noticed when you opened this spreadsheet was the highlighted rectangle; this rectangle marks the *active cell* and is similar to the cursor in word processing. It is the cell with which you are presently working. If you want to work on another cell, you will have to move the highlighted rectangle. You can always tell which cell is the active cell by looking at the extreme left side of the Status bar. In Figure 6–6 you can see the cell address A1 listed as the currently active cell.

Moving the Highlight

It is important that you become adept at moving the highlight in order to complete these worksheets as easily as possible. The following table gives several methods for moving the highlight around the spreadsheet to select different cells. Practice using each of these methods until you feel comfortable with them.

Using the Keyboard

Press	For this result
arrow keys	Moves the highlight one cell in the direction of the arrow
(END)	Moves the highlight to the end of the present line
(HOME)	Moves the highlight to the beginning of the present line
(PGDN)	Displays the next 20 rows of the spreadsheet
(PGUP)	Displays the previous 20 rows of the spreadsheet
(CTRL)-(HOME)	Moves to the beginning of the file
(CTRL)-(END)	Moves to the end of the file

Using the Menu

Another method of moving the highlight is called the "Go To" method, in which you use the menus to specify the cell you wish to activate next. The "Go To" method is very valuable when you want to move to a distant cell. Follow the instructions given below to move to Cell A18 to type your name and today's date:

1. Press: (ALT) to enter the Menu bar.
2. Type: **s** to display the SELECT menu.
3. Type: **g** to select the GO TO option. When the GO TO dialog box appears,
4. Type: **a18** (the cell destination).

Since the Names field should remain empty and <OK> is already highlighted,

5. Press: (ENTER) to complete the move.

The highlight is now in Cell A18 making it the active cell.

Entering Text

The **Formula bar** is the black bar area just below the Menu bar in the upper section of the screen. Whatever you type first appears in the Formula bar. Watch the Formula bar as you complete step 1 that follows.

Note: When you type numbers using the PC keyboard, remember to use the keys at the TOP of the keyboard; use the numeric keypad for cursor movement. When using the AT/XT keyboard, you have separate arrow keys for cursor movement.

1. **Type your name and today's date** to identify your assignment and date of submission.

Correcting Errors

Note that the text appears in the Formula bar but not in the active cell because you have not yet entered the text. If you should make a mistake while typing text, but before it has been entered in the active cell, you can make corrections as follows:

Press	For this result
(BACKSPACE)	to delete the last character typed
(DEL)	to delete the character at the cursor position
(ESC)	to delete the entire entry from the Formula bar

Note: Incidentally, although there is no UNDO feature in the spreadsheet tool of *Works*, (ESC) will still usually take you back to the previous action performed.

When the text in the Formula bar is accurate,

2. Press: (ENTER)   The data in the Formula bar is entered into the Active Cell, A18. If you notice an error now, retype the entry and Press (ENTER) again.

Notice that your name and the date overflow into Column B and perhaps beyond. However, only Column A is considered to be occupied. When a cell is not wide enough to show all the characters it contains, many spreadsheet programs, such as *Works*, will continue to display the characters until an occupied cell is encountered. Since there are no other cells occupied on Row 18, the entire line can be used for displaying your name and date.

Viewing a Label

Do you see the quotation mark (") which *Works* inserted in front of your name in the Formula bar? This identifies the cell as a **label**; that is, descriptive text rather than numbers or formulas. Labels are not used in computations and are automatically left-justified in the cell. All cells beginning with an alphabetic character are presumed to be labels; any cell will be treated as a label if you type a quotation mark before you type the data to be entered into the cell.

 1. Press: (↑) and watch the Formula bar until the highlight reaches Cell A6. Notice that all the entries in this column are labels as evidenced by the quotation mark that appears as the first character in the Formula bar. Notice also that quotation marks do not appear in the spreadsheet itself.

Viewing a Number

All the cells in the area from Cell B6 through Cell I12 and on Row 14 from Columns B though I are **values** of some type. Values can be represented either as simple numerics or as formulas. To view a simple numeric value,

2. Press: (→) **once**.

Sunday's cone/cup sales will be displayed in both the Formula bar and in the active cell. Notice that there is no quotation mark in the Formula bar since this cell contains a numeric value and does not contain a label. Also notice that numeric values align themselves at the right side of a cell.

Viewing a Formula

There is another kind of a value cell used in spreadsheets. It is called a **formula**. A formula cell contains directions for calculating a numeric value to be displayed in that cell. When a cell contains a formula, the calculated value will be displayed in the body of the spreadsheet, but the formula used to make the calculations will be displayed in the Formula bar. There are two kinds of formulas that can be used—user-defined formulas and predefined built-in formulas. The latter are often called **_functions._**

To view a formula,

3. Press: (ALT) to enter the Menu bar.

4. Type: **s** (SELECT dialog box appears).

5. Type: **g** to select the GO TO option.

6. Type: **i12** (that's the LETTER i followed by the number 12).

7. Press: (ENTER) to move the highlight to Cell I12.

Notice that, unlike the other cells you have seen, the displayed value in the highlight looks far different from the contents displayed in the Formula bar. Rather than entering a number in this cell, Chris entered the formula which appears in the Formula bar. Formulas consist of cell addresses together with arithmetic or logical operators. *Works* made the necessary calculations and displayed the resulting calculated value in the cell.

In this particular case, the formula

$$=G12+H12$$

instructs *Works* to make Cell I12 (Total Receipts) equal to the number in Cell G12 (Total Sales) plus the number in Cell H12 (Taxes Collected).

Viewing a Function

Some formulas are used so often that most (if not all) spreadsheet programs include them as **_functions_** so users do not have to build them themselves. Generally speaking, these pre-defined functions save time when dealing with large numbers of adjacent cells. To view an example of a function,

 1. Press: (↓) until the highlight rests in Cell I14.

Remember, you can look at the left side of the Status bar to find out the cell address where the highlight is currently resting.

Again, compare the displayed value in Cell I14 (3,675) with what is displayed in the Formula bar, **=Sum(I6:I12)** —as you can see, the displayed items are very different. The Formula bar contains the function that was used to calculate the value that is displayed in Cell I14. The function instructs *Works* to make Cell I14 (Total Receipts for the week) equal to the sum of the cells in Column I from Cells I6 through I12 (Daily Total Receipts).

Each element of the function has a special meaning, as follows:

=	The equals sign in the Formula bar signifies that a formula or function follows.
SUM	This is the name of one of the pre-defined formulas (functions) provided by *Works* which adds the contents of cells.
( )	The parentheses marks surround the cells with which the function will work.
I6	Cell I6 is the first cell to be added.
:	The colon separates the first cell from the last cell in the range of cells to be used in the function.
I12	Cell I12 is the last cell to be added.

If the SUM function were not available, you could have achieved the same results by using the following formula:

$$= I6+I7+I8+I9+I10+I11+I12$$

There are numerous other functions available; for example, you can use

> *mathematical functions* such as random numbers,
>
> *statistical functions* such as average value,
>
> *logical functions* such as if-then-else, and
>
> *financial functions* such as present value.

See the *Microsoft Works Reference* manual for a comprehensive listing of functions and an explanation of each.

Deleting a Column

Chris has decided that there is no need to separate Pre-Packaged Sales from Hand-Packed Sales. She has asked you to combine both under one heading—Bulk. To do this, you will eliminate the "Pre-pk" column and combine both numbers under the new heading which will replace "Hand-pk".

Before you begin, take a moment to check the Total Sales for the week ($3,673) and Total Receipts ($3,675). Since you will simply be combining the data for two existing columns, these totals should not change.

Remember that you must select (highlight) cells before instructing *Works* to perform actions on those cells. Therefore to delete a column, you will first select the entire column and then tell *Works* what action should be taken on those cells.

1. Press: **arrow** keys to move the highlight to Cell E1, the first cell in the "Pre-pk" column which is to be eliminated.

2. Press: (SHIFT)-(F8) (hold down the (SHIFT) key, press (F8), then release both) to highlight the entire column.

3. Press: (ALT) to enter the Menu bar

4. Type: **e** (EDIT menu).

5. Type: **d** to select DELETE option.

The column disappears. Now you are ready to rename the "Hand-pk" column and enter the revised data for the new column.

Changing Cell Contents

Before changing cell contents, you need to try one more correction method—clearing cells. Sometimes you may make such a mess of an entry that you just want to erase its contents and start over again. To do this easily,

1. Press: **arrow** keys to move the highlight to Cell E4. Look at the Formula bar and you will see that the cell content, "Hand-pk", is displayed.

2. Press: (BACKSPACE) Look at the Formula bar; "Hand-pk" has disappeared from the Formula bar, but it is still showing in Cell E4. To clear Cell E4,

3. Press: (ENTER) Cell E4 is now cleared.

Clearing cells is especially useful when you type data in a cell which should be blank. To enter the new heading for Cell E4,

4. Type: **Bulk**

5. Press: (ENTER)

You are now ready to enter the new values. To replace cell contents, you need not clear the cell first. You may simply type the desired value (it will appear in the Formula bar) and press (ENTER) which will replace the old data with the new. For example, to change Sunday Bulk sales to 75,

6. Press: **arrow** keys to move to Cell E6. The number 51 now displays on the spreadsheet and in the Formula bar.

7. Type: **75** (using the numbers at the top of the keyboard) which is the sum of the previous Pre-packed and Hand-packed sales. Notice that "75" appears in the Formula bar. To enter it on the spreadsheet,

8. Press: (↓)

The Ⓙ acts like the (ENTER) key in that it enters the number into the active cell; but in addition, Ⓙ moves the highlight to the cell below.

9. **Follow steps 7 and 8 above** to enter the remaining values in Column E:

Monday	45
Tuesday	60
Wednesday	77
Thursday	56
Friday	74
Saturday	97

10. Take time now to compare your Total Sales and Total Receipts columns to the previous totals ($3,673 and $3,675 respectively); if they are not the same, check your work to find the error and correct it.

Playing "What If?"

Now that you have completed the worksheet, you are probably still wondering if any time would be saved by using the spreadsheet rather than pencil and paper. The answer would probably be "no" if you used the model you developed (sometimes called a *template*) only once. But if you used it over and over again, you would find yourself saving a considerable amount of time. For example, suppose an error was made in closing on Saturday—one large off-site order for $47 worth of party goods was not recorded because Chris delivered it herself, took the money home, and didn't discover the mistake until today.

If you used the pencil and paper method, you would have to recalculate five items, as follows: (1) Saturday Party sales, (2) Total Sales for Saturday, (3) Total Receipts for Saturday, (4) Total Sales for the week, and (5) Total Receipts for the week. Let's see what you would do using this spreadsheet template:

1. Press: **arrow** keys to move to Cell D12 which contains Saturday Party sales total of $211. (Don't forget to watch the Active Cell Indicator on the left side of the Status bar to help you identify which cell is highlighted.)

2. Type: **258** which increases the previous $211 balance by the $47 error. As you press the key in step 3 below, several of the cells below and to the right of Cell D12 will change. You should focus on Cell D14, the Totals cell for the Party column.

3. Press: (ENTER) and all five calculations you would have had to make manually happen automatically!

You only needed to make one calculation—the other cells which needed correction were automatically updated because those cells all contain formulas or functions which refer directly or indirectly to Cell D12.

Saving the File with a Different Name

By following the instructions in this section you will be able to save your changed file on your data disk under a different name. Then, if you want to work with the original one again you will be able to do so.

1. Press: (ALT) to enter the Menu bar. Since FILE is already highlighted,

2. Press: (ENTER)   The FILE menu will drop down.

3. Type: **a** (to select the SAVE AS... option) The SAVE AS dialog box will appear.

4. **Look at the Current Drive field** (line 2 in the dialog box) **If it does not read A:\, follow steps (a) through (c). Otherwise, continue to step 5.**

   a. Press: (TAB) **one time.** The cursor will move to the Other Drives & Directories box.

   b. Press: (↓) until [-A-] is highlighted.

   c. Press: (ENTER)   The Current Drive field will change to A:\

5. Type: **RECEIPT2** in the File Name field.

6. Press: (ENTER)

The red light will glow on the floppy disk drive as the file is being saved.

Printing a File

Turn on your printer and check that it is ready to print.

1. Press: (ALT) to enter the Menu bar.

2. Type: **p** to select the PRINT menu.

Because spreadsheets are often quite wide, they sometimes do not fit on one page. To ensure that this one does, you will make your left and right margins as small as possible:

3. Type: **L** to select LAYOUT option.

4. Press: (TAB) until the cursor is at the Left Margin line.

5. Type: **0** (that's the number 0).

6. Press: (TAB) to move to the Right Margin line.

7. Type: **0** (that's the number again).

Headers and footers are not needed for this exercise. The next two steps will help you clear those fields if necessary.

8. If text appears in the Header box,

    a. Press: (TAB) until the Header box is highlighted.

    b. Press: (DEL) to remove the unwanted text.

9. If text appears in the Footer box,

    a. Press: (TAB) until the Footer box is highlighted.

    b. Press: (DEL) to remove the unwanted text.

10. Press: (ENTER) to complete the Layout dialog box.

To print the worksheet,

11. Press: (ALT) to enter the Menu bar.

12. Type: **p** (PRINT menu appears). Since PRINT is already highlighted,

13. Press: (ENTER)   The PRINT dialog box appears.

14. Press: (ENTER) to accept the highlighted default setting of one copy.

Review

If time permits, load *Receipts* again and try to make the corrections without looking at the directions.

Summary

Congratulations! You've covered a lot of territory. You should be able to recognize spreadsheets; identify rows, columns, and cells; move the highlight around the spreadsheet; identify labels and columns; enter and delete cells, know the difference between cell content and cell display; and identify formulas and functions.

Quitting *Works*

To quit *Works*, follow the steps below:

▐▮▶   **1.** Press: (ALT) to enter the Menu bar. Since FILE is already highlighted,

2. Press: (ENTER)

3. If a prompt appears asking whether you want to save changes (for example, the margin in the Layout), **press Y**.

4. Type: **cd** to change the Current Directory to the root (main) directory from which you started.

5. **Take your disk out of Drive A and place it in the protective envelope.**

6. **Turn the computer off.**

7 Spreadsheets: Worksheet 2

Setting the Scene

The owner, Chris Hughes, has created a spreadsheet to keep track of payroll. It lists employees alphabetically with their pay rate.

Each week Column D will be updated to include hours worked that week. The last three columns contain formulas and functions which compute each employee's gross pay, the FICA (Social Security) tax deduction, and the net amount of each paycheck. Chris asks you to change the format of all dollar amount columns so that the amounts will be displayed accurately to two decimal points; she also wants you to add a column for Christmas bonuses, and make other improvements to the appearance of the spreadsheet.

In this chapter, you will have the opportunity to

- Insert a column
- Format cells to display values accurate to two decimal places
- Format labels to display centered
- Understand the difference between absolute and relative cell references
- Copy formulas
- Use the Edit function key
- Change column width

Starting *Works* ‖⇒

Figure 7-1

1. Type: **cd\works**
2. Press: (ENTER)
3. Type: **works**
4. Press: (ENTER)

The screen will look similar to Figure 7–1.

Opening a File

A spreadsheet file with which you will work has been prepared and stored on your data disk under the file name *PAYROLL.WKS*. (See Figure 7–2.) The name *Payroll* is intended

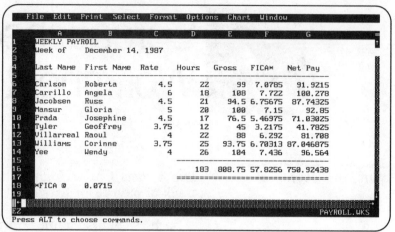

```
    File  Edit  Print  Select  Format  Options  Chart  Window
             A          B           C        D       E       F         G
1   WEEKLY PAYROLL
2   Week of        December 14, 1987
3
4   Last Name    First Name    Rate     Hours   Gross   FICA*    Net Pay
5
6   Carlson      Roberta        4.5      22       99    7.0785   91.9215
7   Carrillo     Angela          6       18      108    7.722    100.278
8   Jacobsen     Russ           4.5      21     94.5   6.75675  87.74325
9   Mansur       Gloria          5       20      100    7.15     92.85
10  Prada        Josephine      4.5      17     76.5   5.46975  71.03025
11  Tyler        Geoffrey      3.75      12       45    3.2175   41.7825
12  Villarreal   Raoul           4       22       88    6.292    81.708
13  Williams     Corinne       3.75      25    93.75   6.70313  87.046875
14  Yee          Wendy           4       26      104    7.436    96.564
15                                      ─────────────────────────────
16                                      183   808.75  57.8256  750.92438
17                                      ═════════════════════════════
18  *FICA @      0.0715
19
20                                                            PAYROLL.WKS
    Press ALT to choose commands.
```

Figure 7-2

to help you remember the type of data stored in the file, and the extension ".WKS" is the standard *Works* file extension for spreadsheet files.

IIII➡ 1. Press: (TAB) until the cursor reaches the <OPEN> option.

2. Press: (ENTER)   The OPEN dialog box will appear. (See Figure 7–3.)

3. Press: (TAB) until the cursor moves to the middle box.

4. Press: (⬇) until [-A-] is highlighted.

5. Insert your data disk into Drive A.

6. Press: (ENTER)   A list of file names will appear in the left-hand box.

7. Press: (TAB) until the cursor moves to the right-hand box.

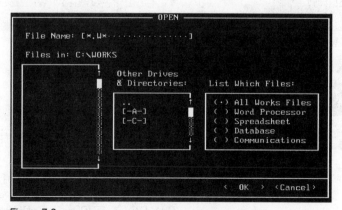

```
                            OPEN
      File Name: [*.W*················]

      Files in: C:\WORKS

                              Other Drives
                              & Directories:     List Which Files:
                              ┌──────────┐
                              │ ..       │      (·) All Works Files
                              │ [-A-]    │      ( ) Word Processor
                              │ [-C-]    │      ( ) Spreadsheet
                              │          │      ( ) Database
                              │          │      ( ) Communications
                              └──────────┘

                                          <  OK  >  <Cancel>
```

Figure 7-3

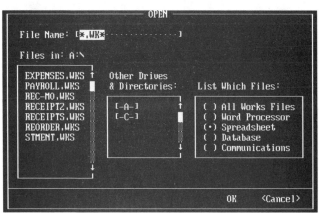

Figure 7-4

8. Press: (↓) to move the cursor to the Spreadsheet option.

9. Press: (ENTER)   Your screen should look similar to Figure 7–4.

10. Press: (TAB) until the cursor is at the left-hand box.

11. Press: (↓) until *PAYROLL.WKS* is highlighted.

12. Press: (ENTER)   The *Payroll* file will appear on the screen.

Inserting a Column

Figure 7-5

To insert a column for the $10 Christmas bonus Chris plans to give each employee this week, you must first select (highlight) the column in which the bonus should appear. When you insert the new column, it will move the present contents of the selected column to the right. To insert the new column labelled Bonus between Hours and Gross,

1. **Move the highlight to Cell E1**, the first cell in the column you wish to use for the Christmas Bonus.

2. Press: (SHIFT)-(F8) to select (highlight) the entire column.

3. Press: (ALT) to enter the Menu bar.

4. Type: **e** to display EDIT menu. (See Figure 7–5.)

The Edit Menu

Notice all the options available for you to use on your selected column. A few of the most frequently used options are MOVE, CLEAR, INSERT, and DELETE. If you used MOVE at this time, the program would erase this column from its present location and insert it in a new location. If you used CLEAR at this time, the contents of this column would be erased and an empty column would remain. If you used DELETE at this point, the entire column would disappear and the remaining columns to the right would fill in the vacated space. INSERT is the option you want to use, so

5. Type: **i** to select the INSERT option. A new blank column appears.

6. Press: ⊙ to deselect the new column.

7. **Move the highlight to Cell E4** where you will type the columnar heading.

8. Type: **Bonus**

9. Press: ⊙ to enter the heading and move down one line.

10. Type: "---------- (that's a quotation mark followed by ten hyphens; the quotation mark informs *Works* that the hyphens which follow are to be treated as text, not as minus signs).

11. Press: ⊙ to Cell E6, Roberta's bonus.

12. Type: **10**

13. Press: (ENTER) to record the $10 bonus for Roberta.

Using the Fill Down and Fill Right Commands

You could continue using steps 12 and 13 to record the $10 bonus for each employee, but there is a faster way—the FILL DOWN command which will copy the contents of the top highlighted cell to the highlighted cells below. With the highlight still in Cell E6,

1. Press: (F8) to signal that the selection is to be extended.

2. Press: ⊙ until the bonus column for all employees is selected, from E6 through E14.

3. **Look at the left side of the Status bar at the bottom of the screen.** It should say E6:E14. If it does not, repeat the selection process until Cells E6 through E14 have been selected.

4. Press: (ALT) to enter the Menu bar.

5. Type: **e** to choose the EDIT menu.

6. Type: **f** to select the FILL DOWN option. The copy is completed.

Now the Bonus column needs to be totalled and some lines need to be extended. You may type it from scratch, but an easier way is to copy the formula for summing hours and the lines above and below it by using the FILL RIGHT function:

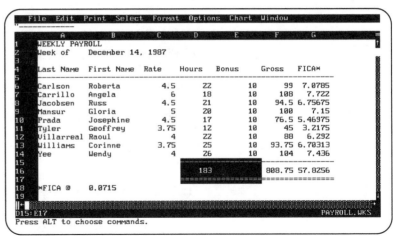

Figure 7-6

⫸

1. Press: **arrow** keys until D15, the line before Total Hours, is highlighted.

2. Press: (F8) to begin extended selection.

3. Press: (→) **once** to extend the highlight from D15 to E15.

4. Press: (↓) **twice** to highlight the three cells from Column D which you want to copy and the three cells in Column E to which the copy is to be made. Your screen should look something like the one in Figure 7–6.

   The Status bar should show D15:E17 as the selected cells.

5. Press: (ALT) to enter the Menu bar.

6. Type: **e** to choose the EDIT menu.

7. Type: **r** to select the FILL RIGHT option. Copy is completed.

8. Press: (↓) to move the cursor to Cell D16.

Relative and Absolute Values

The copy commands are real time-savers and help keep errors to a minimum if you take the time to understand them. The original formula in Cell D16 reads: **=SUM(D6:D14)**. What do you think the copy *Works* made into Cell E16 looks like? Take the time now to compare the original formula to the copy in Cell E16. Notice that *Works* changed all cell references and made them *relative* to position. For example, the formula in Cell D16 adds values in Rows 6 through 14 in Column D. When *Works* copied the formula, it assumed that you also wanted the formula in Cell E16 to add the values in Rows 6 through 14 in its column, Column E—and that's what the formula **=SUM(E6:E14)** does.

You may wonder what you do when you don't want cell addresses to change relative to position. An example would be the computation of FICA taxes in which each employee's gross pay is multiplied by the current FICA rate (see Column G). Although the gross pay of each employee changes, the FICA rate, shown in the bottom left corner of the template, does not. Take a good look at Column G by following the next set of instructions.

⏩ 1. **Use the arrow keys to move to Cell G6.** This is the cell in which FICA taxes are computed for Roberta and which was copied for all other employees.

The formula displayed in the Formula bar looks a little formidable, but is quite simple:

=	Indicates that a formula or function follows
$B	The $ indicates that the following column is not to be changed whenever this formula is copied; this is an ***absolute reference***.
$18	The row number is also an absolute reference and is not to be changed when copied.
*	Indicates multiplication
F6	Because this cell is not set off by dollar signs, it is a relative address; it will be changed relative to its new position when copied.

As you complete the next step, notice how "B18" did not change as the formula was copied, but the row in "F6" was incremented by one each time it was copied down the column.

2. Press: ⬇ and study the change in the formula all the way down to Cell G14.

A simple illustration may help you understand the difference between relative and absolute. Joe Moran invites Mike, a new neighbor, to a party at his home which is just up the street from Mike. If he tells Mike to walk north and stop at the fourth house on the right, he is giving a RELATIVE direction that only applies to Mike. If Joe gave Mike an absolute address, he would tell him that he lives at 125 Ocean Street.

Changing a Formula

Did you happen to notice that the Net Pay did not change when you added the Christmas bonus? Can you guess why? How many formulas need to be changed?

If you guessed that only the formulas in the Gross Pay column need changing, you are right! The instructions in this section will tell you how to do it.

▉➡ **1. Move the highlight to Cell F6.**

2. Look at the Formula bar.

The formula to compute Roberta's pay is incomplete because it does not include the bonus amount. C6 still should be multiplied times D6, but E6 should be added to compute gross pay. To make this change, you may either retype the formula and (ENTER) it or you can edit the formula by following steps 3 through 5 below.

3. Press: (F2) which is the Edit key; the blinking cursor appears at the end of the formula in the Formula bar.

4. Type: **+E6** to complete the formula. Watch the last three columns change as you press the next key.

5. Press: (ENTER) to enter the formula.

Copying a Formula

If you did not see the changes being made, be sure to watch carefully in the next sequence. To copy the formula,

▉➡ **1.** Press: (F8) to signify that you want to select a range of cells.

2. Press: (↓) **eight times** until Cells F6 through F14 are highlighted.

3. Press: (ALT) to enter the Menu bar.

4. Type: **e** to choose the EDIT menu. Be sure to watch the amounts change as you press the next key.

5. Type: **f** to select the FILL DOWN option.

Formatting Numeric Values

Although the amount columns are calculated accurately, they are difficult to read because they are not rounded to the nearest cent—some have no cent amount displayed and others have four or five displayed decimals. To reformat the last four columns,

▉➡ **1. Move the highlight to Cell E6**, the upper left corner of the range you need to highlight.

2. Press: (F8) to indicate you are selecting a range of cells.

3. Press: (↓) until the highlight reaches Cell E16, the total of the Bonus column.

Cell E6 — start selection here

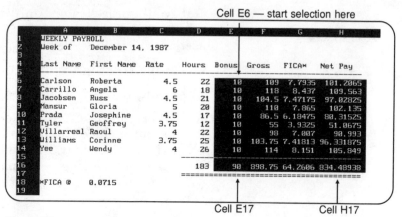

Figure 7-7

Figure 7-8

4. Press: → until the highlight covers Columns E, F, G, and H. Your screen should resemble Figure 7–7.

5. Press: ALT to enter the Menu bar.

6. Type: **t** to choose the FORMAT menu (Figure 7–8).

As you can see, there are many options from which to select. The GENERAL format is the default setting which Chris used when she created the spreadsheet. DOLLAR would appear to be the logical choice, but that option places dollar signs in each cell—and that can be distracting. Financial worksheets are usually formatted to display values accurate to two decimal places through the FIXED format. Therefore,

7. Type: **f** to select the FIXED option. When the DECIMAL dialog box appears,

8. Press: ENTER to accept the default setting of two decimal places.

Much neater, isn't it? Now one more column needs to be reformatted—Column C containing the hourly rates of employees. See if you can remember how to reformat it. If you need help, simply select Cells C6 through C16, then follow steps 5 through 8 above to reformat them.

Formatting Labels

The spreadsheet is looking much better, but some of the columnar headings don't line up directly above the columns—particularly the Hours and Bonus columns. Centering the columnar headings above all amount columns should help.

1. Press: **arrow** keys until Cell C4 (Rate) is highlighted.

2. Press: F8 to signal extended selection.

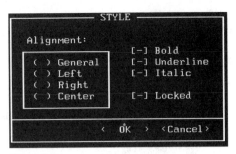

Figure 7-9

3. Press: →) until Cell H4 (Net Pay) is highlighted.

4. Press: (ALT) to enter the Menu bar.

5. Type: **t** (to display FORMAT menu).

6. Type: **s** (to select the STYLE option). STYLE dialog box appears. (See Figure 7–9.)

Note the options available. The alignment block on the left contains the blinking cursor in the default GENERAL format. You move within that block by using the arrow keys. The (TAB) key will move the cursor to the letter styles options and to the action buttons at the bottom of the screen.

7. Press: ↓) until CENTER is selected. Since that is all you need from this dialog box,

8. Press: (ENTER)

Changing Column Width

Since the amounts in Column D take half the space as the others, the spreadsheet's appearance could also be improved by decreasing the width of Column D.

 1. Press: →) to move to Cell D4.

2. Press: (SHIFT)-(F8) to select (highlight) the entire column.

3. Press: (ALT) to enter the Menu bar.

4. Type: **t** to display FORMAT menu.

5. Type: **w** to select WIDTH option. When the WIDTH dialog box appears, the present width of 8 is highlighted. To reduce it to 6,

6. Type: **6**

7. Press: (ENTER) to activate the change.

The default size of columns is 10, so Column E was automatically assigned 10 spaces when you created it. Chris made all amount columns 8 spaces wide except for the Net Pay column which was left at the default of 10. If time permits, see if you can change the width of Column E to 8 spaces.

Identifying Your Work

To identify yourself as the creator of this revision and supply the date of the revision,

▐▶ **1.** Press: **arrow** keys to move to Cell A20.

2. Type your name and today's date.

3. Press: (ENTER)

Printing a File

Figure 7-10

Turn on your printer and check that it is ready to print.

▐▶ **1.** Press: (ALT) to enter the Menu bar.

2. Type: **p** to select the PRINT menu.

Because spreadsheets are often wide, they sometimes do not fit on one page. To ensure that this one does, you will make your left and right margins as small as possible:

3. Type: **L** to select the LAYOUT option.

4. Press: (TAB) to move to the LEFT MARGIN line.

5. Type: **0** (that's the number 0).

6. Press: (TAB) to move to the RIGHT MARGIN line.

7. Type: **0** (that's the number again).

Since headers and footers are not needed for this exercise, the next two steps will help you clear those fields.

8. If text appears in the Header box,

   a. Press: (TAB) until the Header box is highlighted.

   b. Press: (DEL) to remove the unwanted text.

9. If text appears in the Footer box,

   a. Press: (TAB) until the Footer box is highlighted.

   b. Press: (DEL) to remove the unwanted text.

10. Press: (ENTER) to complete the LAYOUT dialog box.

To print the worksheet,

11. Press: (ALT) to enter the Menu bar.

12. Type: **p** to choose PRINT menu. When the PRINT dialog box appears,

13. Press: (ENTER) since PRINT is already highlighted. When the next dialog box appears,

14. Press: (ENTER) to accept the default settings and to start printing.

Saving the File with a Different Name

Now that you have completed all the changes and the spreadsheet looks so great, you should save it with a different name. Follow these instructions.

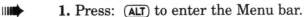

1. Press: (ALT) to enter the Menu bar.

2. Press: (ENTER)   The FILE menu will drop down.

3. Type: **a** to select SAVE AS option. When the SAVE AS dialog box appears,

4. Type: **Pay2**

5. **Look at the Current Drive field** (line 2 in the dialog box). **If it does not read A:\, follow steps a through c. Otherwise, continue to step 6.**

   a. Press: (TAB) **one time.** The cursor will move to the Other Drives & Directories box.

   b. Press: (↓) until [-A-] is highlighted.

   c. Press: (ENTER)   The Current Drive field will change to A:\

6. Press: (ENTER)   The red light will glow on the floppy disk drive as the file is being saved.

Review

If time permits, load *PAYROLL.WKS* again and try to make the corrections without looking at the directions.

Summary

Congratulations! The payroll spreadsheet is now ready to submit to Chris and you have successfully added a column, formatted values, formatted labels, studied the difference between absolute and relative cell references, copied formulas, used the Edit function key, and changed column width.

Quitting *Works*

1. Press: (ALT) to enter the Menu bar. Since FILE is already highlighted,

2. Press: (ENTER)

3. Type: **cd** to change the Current Directory to the root (main) directory from which you started.

4. **Take your disk out of Drive A and place it in the protective envelope.**
5. **Turn the computer off.**

8 Spreadsheets: Worksheet 3

Setting the Scene

As you can imagine, The Ice Cream Factory does not have space to stock more than one week's supply of ice cream at a time. As a result, Chris has created a rough draft of a form which will standardize the reordering process and prepare an easy-to-read report. It is shown in Figure 8–1.

In this chapter, you will have the opportunity to work with the rough draft of this form as you

- Center a heading
- Study the Date format
- Insert a row
- Study the effect of adding cells at the end of a range which is used in formulas
- Create formulas and copy them
- Center columnar data under its heading
- Protect cells

```
 File   Edit   Print   Select   Format   Options   Chart   Window

        A                B                    C          D            E
1                                        REORDER FORM
2
3   Date:      Jan 5, 1988
4
5   Item No.   Description           No. Needed  In Inventory No. to Order
6   ------------------------------------------------------------------------
7        101  Vanilla                    15          2              13
8        102  Chocolate                   7          2         FORMULA
9        103  Strawberry                  7          1         FORMULA
10       104  Almond Chocolate            5          1         FORMULA
11       105  Cherry Vanilla              1          0         FORMULA
12       106  Praline 'n Almond           4          2         FORMULA
13       107  Kona Coffee                 4          1         FORMULA
14       108  French Vanilla              5          2         FORMULA
15       109  German Chocolate            3          1         FORMULA
16       110  Peaches 'n Cream            1          1         FORMULA
17       111  Caramel Crunch              3          0
18  ------------------------------------------------------------------------
19            TOTALS                     52         13         FORMULA

A1                                                              REORDER.WKS
Press ALT to choose commands.
```

Figure 8-1

Starting *Works*

Figure 8-2

Follow the directions below to load *Works*:

1. Type: **cd\works**

2. Press: (ENTER)

3. Type: **works**

4. Press: (ENTER)

The screen will look like Figure 8–2.

Opening a File

A spreadsheet file has already been prepared for you to work with. The file is stored on your data disk under the file name *REORDER.WKS*.

1. Press: (TAB) **two times** to select <OPEN>.

2. Press: (ENTER)   The OPEN dialog box will appear. (See Figure 8–3.)

3. Press: (TAB) until the cursor moves to the middle box.

4. Press: (↓) until [-A-] becomes highlighted.

5. **Insert your data disk in Drive A.**

6. Press: (ENTER)   A list of file names will appear in the left-hand box.

7. Press: (TAB) until the cursor moves to the right-hand box.

8. Press: (↓) to select the Spreadsheet application.

9. Press: (ENTER)   Your screen should look similar to Figure 8–4.

10. Press: (TAB) until the cursor moves to the left-hand box.

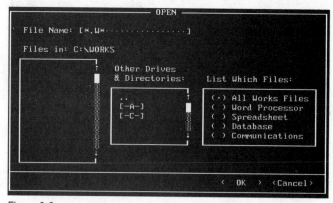

Figure 8-3

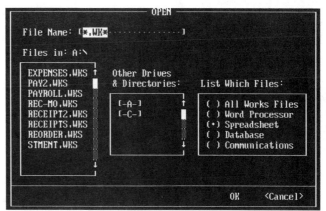
Figure 8-4

11. Press: ⊕ until *REORDER.WKS* is highlighted.

12. Press: (ENTER)   The *Reorder* file will appear on the screen.

Centering a Heading

Although you cannot select a range of cells and center one heading in the middle of the range, you can perform a "quick and dirty" center by visually placing the title where you think it would look best. For example, to place the heading "Reorder Form" so it looks centered,

1. **Move the highlight to Cell A1.** This is the present location of the report title "Reorder Form".

2. Press: (ALT) to enter the Menu bar.

3. Type: **e** (to choose the EDIT menu). Since MOVE is already highlighted,

4. Press: (ENTER)   A message appears at the bottom of the screen asking you to "Select new location and press ENTER..."

5. Press: → to move the highlight to Cell C1.

6. Press: (ENTER) to complete the move.

Inserting a Blank Row

Although the heading looks improved, now it appears as if there should be a horizontal row inserted to separate the heading and date lines.

1. Press: ⊕ to move to the date line.

2. Press: (CTRL)-(F8)   The entire row will be selected.

3. Press: (ALT) to enter the Menu bar.

4. Type: **e** to choose EDIT menu.

5. Type: **i** to select the INSERT option. The insert operation is now complete.

Understanding the Date Format

Works interprets and records dates as values so that you can make calculations using them—that is why the date displays on the right side of Cell B3. You can improve the appearance of the form by moving the date to the left side of the cell, as follows:

1. Press: **arrow** keys to move the highlight to Cell B3.

2. Press: (ALT) to enter the Menu bar.

3. Type: **t** for FORMAT menu.

4. Type: **s** to select STYLE option. When the STYLE dialog box appears,

5. Press: (↓) until LEFT is selected. Since the rest of the screen is acceptable and <OK> is highlighted,

6. Press: (ENTER) to record your selection.

Inserting a Row at the End of a Range

Chris plans to introduce a new flavor (Caramel Crunch) next week, and estimates that three containers will be needed in your store. You must add this item to your *Reorder* file, but before inserting this flavor as Item No. 111, you wisely decide to study the potential effect of adding this row.

1. Use the arrow keys to move to Cell C18 where "52" is displayed.

Deleting rows and columns seldom causes problems in spreadsheet development. However, inserting sometimes can. For example, look at this summing function in Cell C18: **=SUM(C7:C16).** This function will work if you insert a row anywhere *between* Cells C7 and C16. However, it will not work in many spreadsheet programs if you insert a row *before* C7 or *after* C16—those cells would be beyond the range named in the existing formula. In cases such as this, the range would have to be extended to C17.

To better understand this concept, you will deliberately make a mistake and insert a new row on Row 17 so you can observe what happens.

2. Press: (↑) to move to Row 17, the row on which the new flavor will be inserted.

3. Press: (CTRL)-(F8) to select (highlight) the entire row.

4. Press: (ALT) to enter the Menu bar.

5. Type: **e** to choose EDIT menu.

6. Type: **i** for INSERT option.

7. Press: (←) to move the highlight to Cell A17.

8. Type: **111** (the Item number for the new flavor).

9. Press: (TAB) to enter the number and move to Cell B17.

10. Type: **Caramel Crunch** (the name of the new flavor).

11. Press: (TAB) to enter the flavor and move to Cell C17.

12. Type: **3** to enter the number Chris wants on hand.

13. Press: (TAB) to enter the number and move to Cell D17.

14. Type: **0** (since you have none in inventory at this time).

15. Press: (ENTER) to enter the number and stay in the same cell.

16. Look at Cell C19.

As you can see, the value displayed as the total number needed is still 52; you know it should have increased by three. To go back to correct the formula,

17. Press the arrow keys to move the highlight to Cell C19.

18. Look at the Formula bar.

As you can see, the formula did not adjust to include the new cell. Since cells which do not contain values or references to values are ignored by the SUM function, can you think of how the SUM function now in Cell C19 could be changed to allow for future additions? Here is how it can be done:

19. Type: **=SUM(C6:C18)**

20. Press: (ENTER)

Cell C18 does not contain a value (it contains hyphens), therefore it is ignored by the SUM function. If you like, try inserting another row for your favorite flavor and verify that the new formula will include your new row in its range.

Now you must copy the summing formula to Cells D19 and E19, therefore,

21. Press: (F8) to signal extended selection.

22. Press: (→) **twice** to highlight Cells C19 through E19.

23. Press: (ALT) to enter the Menu bar.

24. Type: **e** for EDIT menu.

25. Type: **r** to select FILL RIGHT option. The copy is now complete.

Creating Formulas

As you can see, Column E ("Number to Order") is missing its formulas. To insert a formula which will print the difference between Columns C and D (the "Number Needed" and "In Inventory"),

1. Use the arrow keys to move to Cell E7.

2. Type: **=C7-D7** (this is the formula that will compute the number to be ordered).

3. Press: (ENTER) to enter the formula. The difference, 13, is displayed in the active cell.

Copying another Formula

By now you know how to copy Cell E7 down the length of the entire column. In case you need a review of this function:

1. Press: (F8) to extend the selection to a range of cells.

2. Press: (↓) until Cells E7 through E17 are highlighted.

3. Press: (ALT) to enter the Menu bar.

4. Type: **e** to select the EDIT menu.

5. Type: **f** to select the FILL DOWN option.

Centering Columns of Data under Headings

Because labels are automatically aligned on the left edge of a column and numbers are automatically aligned on the right edge, Columns A, C, D, and E do not look well balanced. A simple way to correct this situation is to center both the headings and the data in those cells. Begin with the large block of cells marked by Cell C5 in the upper left corner and E19 in the lower right. Figure 8–5 shows the range of cells to be selected.

1. Use the arrow keys to move to Cell C5.

2. Press: (F8) to indicate a range of cells is being selected.

3. Press: (↓) until Cell C19 is highlighted.

4. Press: (→) until Cell E19 is highlighted.

5. Press: (ALT) to enter the Menu bar.

6. Type: **t** for FORMAT menu.

7. Type: **s** for STYLE option. The STYLE dialog box will appear.

This is the block of cells you will work with ⌐

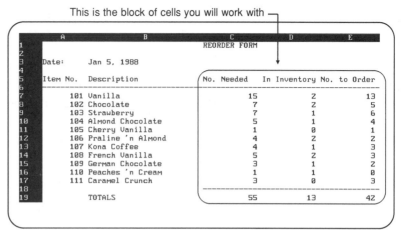

Figure 8-5

8. Press: (⤓) until CENTER is selected.

9. Press: (ENTER) to complete the reformatting.

Notice that the numbers are now left-aligned. The proper format for numbers is right alignment. On your own, change the selected block back to right alignment.

Another Try at Centering Data

See if you can reformat Column A by yourself. If you need a review:

1. **Use the arrow keys** to move to Cell A5.

2. Press: (F8) to indicate a range of cells is being selected.

3. Press: (⤓) until Cell A17 is highlighted.

4. Press: (ALT) to enter the Menu bar.

5. Type: **t** (FORMAT menu).

6. Type: **s** (STYLE dialog box appears).

7. Press: (⤓) until CENTER is selected.

8. Press: (ENTER) to complete the reformatting.

Identifying Your Work

To identify yourself as the creator of this revision and supply the date of the revision,

1. Press: **arrow** keys to move to Cell A20.

2. **Type your name and today's date.**

3. Press: (ENTER)

Protecting Cells

Whenever you have any data, especially complex formulas, that you do not want anyone to accidentally destroy, you should *protect* the cells in which they appear. If anyone tries to enter data in protected cells, the computer will display an appropriate message. In this particular template, you and Chris probably do not want anyone tampering with your formulas in Column E and Row 19. To add protection to those cells:

1. **Use the arrow keys** to highlight Cell E7.

2. Press: (F8) to indicate a range of cells is being selected.

3. Press: (↓) until Cell E17 is highlighted.

4. Press: (ALT) to enter the Menu bar.

5. Type: **o** (that's the letter "o" to choose the OPTIONS menu).

6. Type: **p** to select the PROTECT option. Although it doesn't appear that anything happened, you should not be able to type anything in those cells.

7. Press: (↓) to deselect the block and move to Cell E8.

8. Type: **88**

9. Press: (ENTER) An ERROR dialog box appears stating "Locked cells cannot be changed". To indicate that you read the message,

10. Press: (ENTER)

Saving the File with a Different Name

By following the instructions in this section you will be able to save your completed *Reorder* spreadsheet file on your data disk under a different name. Then, if you want to work with the original one again you will be able to do so.

1. Press: (ALT) to enter the Menu bar.

2. Press: (ENTER) The FILE menu will drop down.

3. Type: **a** to select SAVE AS... option. When SAVE AS dialog box appears,

4. **Look at the Current Drive field (line 2 in the dialog box).** If it does not read A:\ follow steps a through c. Otherwise, continue to step 5.

   a. Press: (TAB) until the cursor moves to the Other Drives & Directories box.

   b. Press: (↓) until [-A-] appears and is highlighted.

    c. Press: (ENTER)   The Current Drive field will change to A:\.

5. Type: **Reord2**   The name will appear in the File Name field.

6. Press: (ENTER)   The red light will glow on the floppy disk drive as the file is being saved.

Printing a File

The instructions in this section will help you print out the spreadsheet you just completed.

▮▮▮▶ **1. Turn on your printer and check that it is ready to print.**

2. Press: (ALT) to enter the Menu bar.

3. Type: **p** to select the PRINT menu.

To ensure that this spreadsheet will fit on one page, you need to make your left and right margins as small as possible.

4. Type: **L** to select LAYOUT option.

5. Press: (TAB) until the cursor is at the Left Margin line.

6. Type: **0** (that's the number 0).

7. Press: (TAB) to move to the Right Margin line.

8. Type: **0** (that's the number 0 again).

9. Press: (ENTER) to complete the LAYOUT dialog box.

To print the worksheet,

10. Press: (ALT) to enter the Menu bar.

11. Type: **p** (PRINT menu appears). Since PRINT is already highlighted,

12. Press: (ENTER)   The PRINT dialog box appears.

13. Press: (ENTER) to accept the highlighted default setting of one copy.

Review

If time permits, load *REORDER.WKS* again and try to make the corrections without looking at the directions.

Summary

Congratulations! The *Reorder* spreadsheet is now complete and you have successfully centered a heading, inserted a row, created new formulas, centered columnar data, and protected cells.

Quitting *Works*

Follow these directions to quit *Works*:

▐▌▶ 1. Press: (ALT) to enter the Menu bar. Since FILE is already highlighted,

2. Press: (ENTER)

3. Type: **cd** to change the Current Directory to the root (main) directory from which you started.

4. **Take your disk out of Drive A and place it in the protective envelope.**

5. **Turn the computer off.**

9

Spreadsheet Shortcuts, Charting, and Special Features

Setting the Scene

Are you ready to try out other spreadsheet features? How about some shortcuts? In order to graphically demonstrate to Chris how expenses were distributed in January, you may wish to use your computer to create a chart. In this chapter, you will learn to

- Use keyboard shortcuts for spreadsheets
- Create a bar chart
- Format cells
- Display formulas in cells
- Print selected cells
- Learn about functions and If Statements

As in Chapter 5, this concluding chapter on spreadsheets assumes prior experience with the worksheets on this function. Ready for the challenge?

Spreadsheet Shortcuts

Following are shortcuts for some of the most commonly used spreadsheet functions. This is not a complete list. Consult the *Microsoft Works Reference* manual for further information.

Selection Shortcuts

To select	Press these keys
A row	CTRL-F8
A column	SHIFT-F8
An entire file	CTRL-SHIFT-F8 (You do not have to be at the beginning of the file.)

Other Shortcuts

To do this	Press these keys	Comments
Go To	(F5)	Type destination cell (e.g., E5, then press (ENTER))
Go Home	(CTRL)-(HOME)	Puts cursor at the beginning of the file
Go To End	(CTRL)-(ENTER)	Puts cursor at the end of the file
Edit	(F2)	Puts blinking cursor on formula line; backspace to delete character(s); type in correction
Copy	(SHIFT)-(F3)	Copies selection to new location

Charting

Note: In order to complete this exercise, a graphics card must be installed in your computer.

There are two ways of charting data from a *Works* spreadsheet: (1) speed charting, or (2) starting from scratch. You can use speed charting for this exercise since the categories and legend names in the spreadsheet you are to chart are adjacent to each other.

In speed charting, the default is set for a bar chart which displays vertical boxes or bars arranged side by side. The bottom horizontal line, or *X-axis*, shows the categories used to classify the data, such as days, months, fiscal years, ages, products, etc. The left vertical line, or *Y-axis*, is a scale representing units of measurement, such as dollar amounts, number of items, or population figures.

Speed charting creates the Y-series based on·the shape of the selected range:

Using speed charting with the file shown in Figure 9–1 will result in a chart in which the words in the first column appear along the horizontal axis (X-axis) and the numbers in the second column appear on the vertical (Y-axis).

The speed chart created from the above file would appear as shown in Figure 9–2.

When you use the speed charting option with more than one column of numbers, *Works* will create a bar for each column. In the example shown in Figure 9–3, the vertical (Y-axis) will be January. The items will be placed along the horizontal (X-axis) and *Works* will display the spreadsheet data (Figure 9-3) as shown in Figure 9–4.

```
Payroll  . . . . . . . 1529.44
Ice Cream . . . . . 6982.00
Other Foods . . . 2322.00
Rent  . . . . . . . . . 1000.00
Utilities  . . . . . . . 525.00
Insurance . . . . . . 120.00
Payroll Tax . . . . . 148.36
```

Figure 9-1

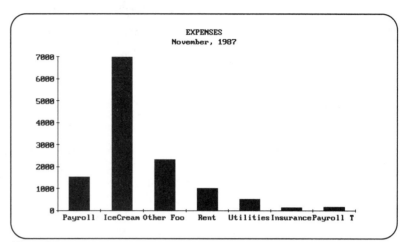

Figure 9-2

Month	Cone/Cup	Fountn.	Party	Bulk
January	7,468	3,252	4,526	2,250

Figure 9-3

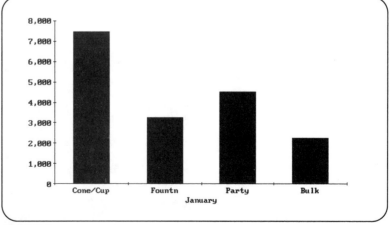

Figure 9-4

To Create a Speed Chart

1. Load the file entitled *STMENT.WKS*.

2. Select Cells B7 through D13.

3. Press: (ALT) to enter Menu bar.

4. Type: **c** to select CHART menu.

5. Type: **n** to select NEW option.

You are now in the Chart Screen (you should see the word "Chart" in the Status bar).

You could now specify the type of chart desired by using the FORMAT menu; however, since we will be using the default, which is the bar option, you will skip that step. (You may enter the Menu bar and look at the various chart options if you like, then press (ESC) to continue with speed charting.)

To Create a Chart Title

1. Press: (ALT) to enter the Menu bar.

2. Type: **d** to select DATA menu.

3. Type: **t** to select TITLES option.

4. Type: **EXPENSES** for the Chart Title line.

5. Press: (TAB) to the Subtitle line.

6. Type: **November, 1987**

7. Press: (ENTER)

To View a Chart

1. Press: (ALT) to enter the Menu bar.

2. Type: **c** to select CHART menu.

3. Type: **v** to select VIEW CHART.

4. Press: (ESC) to leave the VIEW CHART screen.

To Save a Chart

1. Press: (F10) to return to the spreadsheet screen.

2. Press: (ALT) to enter the Menu bar. Since FILE is already highlighted,

3. Press: (ENTER)

4. Type: **s** to select the SAVE option. Since you did not change anything on the spreadsheet, you do not need a new name.

Charts are saved as a part of the spreadsheet file. You will not see the chart listed when you open a file, but it will be included in the CHART menu of that spreadsheet.

To Delete a Chart

If for any reason you want to eliminate a chart (for example, if an error was made or the chart is outdated), follow these steps to delete that chart from the spreadsheet file.

1. Press: (ALT) to enter the Menu bar.

2. Type: **c** to select the CHART menu.

3. Type: **c** (the CHARTS dialog box appears).

4. Press: ⊕ if necessary to select the unwanted chart.

5. Press: (TAB) until the DELETE option is selected.

6. Press: (ENTER) *Works* will ask you to verify the deletion.

7. Press: (ENTER) to verify.

Other Common Spreadsheet Features

Formatting Numbers with Different Options

You can change the appearance of the numeric values in a cell by changing the cell's format. There are seven numeric formats listed in the Format menu: General, Fixed, Dollar, Comma, Percent, Exponential, Logical. If you type a number in a cell without formatting the cell, *Works* uses the General format for displaying the entire number. To change the formatting,

1. Select the cell(s) to be formatted.

2. Choose the FORMAT menu.

3. Select the appropriate option.

4. Type the number of decimal places desired in the NUMBER OF DECIMALS text box.

5. Press (ENTER)

Showing Formula(s)

1. Choose the OPTION menu.

2. Select the SHOW FORMULA option.

The formula(s) will show in place of the figures. (Cells may change in width to accommodate the formula).

Printing Options

At times you may want to print only a portion of your spreadsheet. You can do so as follows:

1. Select the portion of spreadsheet to be printed.

2. Choose the PRINT menu, SET PRINT AREA option.

3. Choose the PRINT menu, PRINT option. When the PRINT dialog box appears, accept default of 1 for Number of Copies.

4. Press (ENTER)

Character Formatting

To use the Bold or Underline feature, select the word(s) to be formatted, then:

1. Choose the FORMAT menu, STYLE option.

2. In the ALIGNMENT dialog box, use the ⬇ to choose desired option.

3. Use (TAB) to move to BOLD, UNDERLINE, ITALIC. Use ⬆ to place an X in desired option. When all options have been checked,

4. Press (ENTER)

If Statement

The *If Statement* can be used in situations where a cell's content would be contingent upon the content of another cell. For example, the figures that follow show an If Statement on a reorder form (see Figures 9-5 and 9-6).

As Displayed

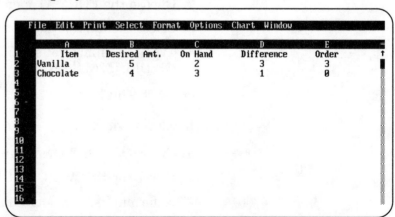

Figure 9-5

As Stored

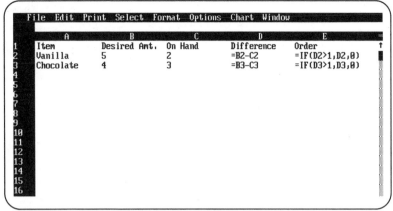

	A	B	C	D	E
	Item	Desired Amt.	On Hand	Difference	Order
1					
2	Vanilla	5	2	=B2-C2	=IF(D2>1,D2,0)
3	Chocolate	4	3	=B3-C3	=IF(D3>1,D3,0)

Figure 9-6

As you can see, the formulas in Column D subtract the supply on hand from the amount desired. Suppose, however, that you did not want to reorder unless you had used *more* than one container. The If Statement in Column E does this for you:

=IF (D2>1,D2,0)   If Cell D2 is greater than 1, then the contents of D2 will be printed in E2; if not, 0 will appear in Cell E2.

Summary

You have been exposed to many of the tools available when using spreadsheets. To learn more about the *Works* spreadsheet tool, choose the WINDOW menu and select either the HELP INDEX or the TUTORIAL INDEX, or you could refer to the *Works* manual.

10 Database: Worksheet 1

Introduction to Database Management

Databases are large collections of related data. Two databases with which you may be familiar are the telephone directory (a collection of names together with addresses and phone numbers) and a file of recipes (a collection of recipe titles together with the ingredients and method of preparation).

Databases are made up of *records* that describe each item in the collection (names in the case of the telephone directory or each recipe in the case of the recipe file).

Each record is composed of a group of *fields* (for example, a name field, address field, and phone number field in the case of the telephone directory, or a type field, ingredients field, and method field in the case of the recipe file).

When you want to find a record in a database, you must search through all the records until you find the one you want. Obviously, the manner in which the records are organized has a major effect on how easy it is to find one specific record. In searching the telephone directory, you know the name and wish to locate the telephone number. For that reason, the telephone database is organized alphabetically by name. Such organization makes it easy for the user to locate a particular person. Suppose, however, that you did not know the name — that all you knew was a telephone number, and it was your desire to find out the name of the person or firm that belonged to that number. Using the telephone book example, if you find a phone number on a scratch pad, it would be virtually impossible for you to find the owner using the traditional telephone book.

When a database is stored on a computer using a database program, you are not limited to searching through the data in just one way. Using a computerized database you can search by name, address, or phone number. You can also view the database as individual records on the screen, or as a list showing all records (or just certain selected records). In some cases you may be able to move the database records into word processing documents and thus create informative reports. Some database programs also include the capability of doing calculations on certain fields.

In the following chapters, you will be working with the database portion of *Microsoft Works*. The worksheets contain instructions that will allow you to retrieve a database file from your data disk, change some data, and then create a new file. When you complete the worksheets, you should be able to create a simple database of your own, just as you would when trying out a program you might want to purchase. Remember, these worksheets are designed to just get you started!

Setting the Scene

In order to manage the Ice Cream Factory efficiently, Chris Hughes has created a simple database file of information about the employees.

As well as keeping track of addresses, phone numbers, and marital status of each employee, the database can be used for such things as creating work schedules and identifying employees in line for raises.

In completing this chapter, you will:

- Recognize fields and records
- View a file by Form and by List
- Perform numeric and alphabetic searches
- Sort records
- Enter new data
- Add a field to a record
- Add a record

Starting *Works*

Follow the directions below to load *Works*:

Figure 10-1

1. **Follow the directions for installing *Microsoft Works* onto your hard disk** if you have not already done so.

2. Type: **cd\works** to change the Current Directory to the *Works* directory.

3. Press: (ENTER)

4. Type: **works**

5. Press: (ENTER)

The screen will look like Figure 10–1.

Opening a File

A database file with which you can work has already been prepared. The file is stored on your data disk under the file name *PROFILE.WDB*. The name *Profile* is intended to help you remember the type of data stored in the file, and the extension ".WDB" is the standard *Works* file extension for database files.

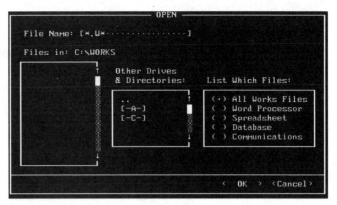

Figure 10-2

1. Press: (TAB) until the cursor moves to <OPEN> option.

2. Press: (ENTER) and the OPEN dialog box will appear. (See Figure 10–2.)

3. Press: (TAB) until the cursor moves to the middle box.

4. Press: ⊕ until the [-A-] becomes highlighted.

5. **Insert your data disk in Drive A.**

6. Press: (ENTER) A list of file names will appear in the left-hand box.

7. Press: (TAB) until the cursor moves to the right-hand box.

8. Press: ⊕ until the cursor moves to the DATABASE line.

9. Press: (ENTER) Your screen should look similar to Figure 10–3.

10. Press: (TAB) until the cursor moves to the left-hand box.

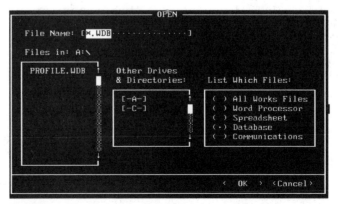

Figure 10-3

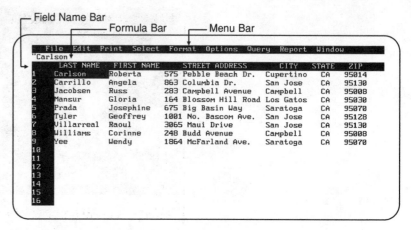

Field Name Bar

Formula Bar

Menu Bar

	LAST NAME	FIRST NAME	STREET ADDRESS	CITY	STATE	ZIP
1	Carlson	Roberta	575 Pebble Beach Dr.	Cupertino	CA	95014
2	Carrillo	Angela	863 Columbia Dr.	San Jose	CA	95130
3	Jacobsen	Russ	283 Campbell Avenue	Campbell	CA	95008
4	Mansur	Gloria	164 Blossom Hill Road	Los Gatos	CA	95030
5	Prada	Josephine	675 Big Basin Way	Saratoga	CA	95070
6	Tyler	Geoffrey	1001 No. Bascom Ave.	San Jose	CA	95128
7	Villarreal	Raoul	3065 Maui Drive	San Jose	CA	95130
8	Williams	Corinne	248 Budd Avenue	Campbell	CA	95008
9	Yee	Wendy	1864 McFarland Ave.	Saratoga	CA	95070

Figure 10-4

11. Press: ⬇ to highlight file name *PROFILE.WDB*.

12. Press: (ENTER) and the *PROFILE.WDB* file will appear on the screen as shown in Figure 10–4.

Viewing a File in a List

Notice that the Menu bar is very similar to those used in Word Processing and Spreadsheets. The ***Formula bar*** acts as it does in the Spreadsheet screen; you use it to enter into and edit the contents of the active cell. The screen itself displays a portion of the database in ***List format*** — all ***records*** (each employee and information relating to him/her) occupy one line each and are listed one under the other. The ***field*** names (the items of information that are available for each employee) are strung across the top of the document.

The List screen lets you work with a database much like you worked with spreadsheets in the prior section. Viewing your database in list form enables you to see many records at one time and therefore is very handy when making comparisons or getting an overall picture of what records are included in the database. It is rather cumbersome to use, however, when there are a large number of fields or when you want to analyze all the items in one record. At those times, you may want to view your records individually.

Viewing a File through Forms

As stated above, one drawback of the list screen is that all the data about each record may not be visible. In this example, there are thirteen fields (columns in the List screen). To see all the information about Roberta Carlson, it is easier to use the Form screen.

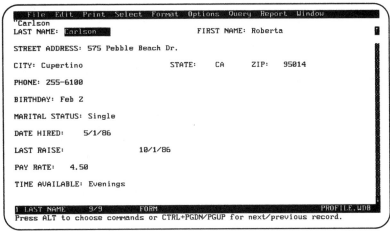

```
      File Edit Print Select Format Options Query Report Window
"Carlson
LAST NAME: Carlson                    FIRST NAME: Roberta                    ▊

STREET ADDRESS: 575 Pebble Beach Dr.

CITY: Cupertino              STATE:   CA      ZIP:    95014

PHONE: 255-6100

BIRTHDAY: Feb 2

MARITAL STATUS: Single

DATE HIRED:    5/1/86

LAST RAISE:               10/1/86

PAY RATE:   4.50

TIME AVAILABLE: Evenings



 1 LAST NAME     9/9          FORM                          PROFILE.WDB
Press ALT to choose commands or CTRL+PGDN/PGUP for next/previous record.
```

Figure 10-5

To display the file one record at a time so all the information about each record can be viewed at once,

1. Press: (ALT) to enter the Menu bar.

2. Type: **o** (the letter "o"). The OPTIONS menu appears.

3. Type: **v** (to select the VIEW FORM option). A screen similar to Figure 10–5 will appear. Notice the word FORM in the Status bar at the bottom of the screen.

The information contained in the Form format is identical to the information contained in the List format. The two formats are just arranged in different ways. Whereas the List format was more like the telephone book listing, the Form format is more like a recipe card. You can flip back and forth through your "cards" as follows:

Press	**For this result**
(CTRL)-(PGUP)	Moves to the previous record
(CTRL)-(PGDN)	Moves to the next record
(CTRL)-(HOME)	Moves to the first record
(CTRL)-(END)	Moves to the last record in the file which is always a blank record.

To switch back to the List screen,

1. Press: (ALT) to enter the Menu bar.

2. Type: **o** to select the OPTIONS menu.

3. Type: **v** to select the VIEW LIST option.

Notice that you used the same procedure to toggle between the Form and List screens. Practice it a few times; you will be using it often to get from one view to the other.

Querying the Database

One of the new Menu bar items is the QUERY, or question, option. Querying lets you display all the records that match certain criteria. For example, suppose an employee who was to work in the afternoon calls in sick. You can ask for all employees who are available to work the afternoon shift by following the steps given in this section. (You should still be in the List form; if you are not, refer to the steps in the previous exercise.)

➡ 1. Press: (ALT) to enter the Menu bar.

2. Type: **q** to choose the QUERY menu. (See Figure 10–6.)

Since DEFINE is already highlighted,

3. Press: (ENTER) to select the DEFINE option.

Figure 10-6

A blank form screen appears with QUERY displayed in the *Status bar* at the bottom of the screen. You will use this screen to define your query — a request for employees available to work in the afternoon.

4. Press: (TAB) until the highlight reaches the TIME AVAIL-ABLE field.

5. Type: **afternoons** (you may use upper- or lower-case letters).

6. Press: (ENTER) to record the criteria.

7. Press: (F10) to apply the query. A list of only those employees who work in the afternoons will be listed. Unfortunately, the TIME AVAILABLE field is the last field and therefore does not show on the screen. You must complete step 8 to view the TIME AVAILABLE field and check the accuracy of the computer's search.

8. Press: (END) Now you can see that all the records listed show a TIME AVAILABLE field of Afternoons.

To exit from the QUERY mode:

➡ 1. Press: (ALT) to enter the Menu bar.

2. Type: **q** to choose the QUERY menu.

3. Type: **a** to select SHOW ALL RECORDS option. The full list should now be displayed.

Entering New Data

A new employee has been hired recently and needs to be added to the database. You will find it easier to enter the complete records for the employee on a Form screen. Since you are in the List view, return to the Form view:

▐▐▶ 1. Press: (ALT) to enter the Menu bar.

2. Type: **o** (the letter "o" for the OPTIONS menu).

3. Type: **v** to select the VIEW FORM option.

To move to the first blank form:

4. Press: (CTRL)-(END)   (Hold down (CTRL), press (END), then release both.)

The active cell is a highlighted rectangle. As you type data into the field, notice that the text will appear in the Formula bar. When you press (ENTER), the text will also appear in the form itself. With the highlight in the LAST NAME field,

5. Type: **Hirvonen**

As you can see, Hirvonen appears in the Formula bar but not on the Form itself. If you make a mistake, you can still use the the (BACKSPACE) and (DEL) keys to erase errors. Assume for a moment that you typed the incorrect name and wanted to quickly erase the entire cell. Remember how?

6. Press: (ESC) which clears the Formula bar since the text was not yet entered.

Now that you know how to correct any errors you may make, let's begin again:

7. Type: **Hirvonen**

8. Press: (TAB) to enter Hirvonen and move to the next field. If you now discover a mistake in the last name, you must move back to that field and either retype or use the (F2) Edit key as in the Spreadsheet section.

9. Type: **Pia**

10. Press: (TAB) to move to the STREET ADDRESS field.

Complete filling in the form using the following data:

LAST NAME:	Hirvonen
FIRST NAME:	Pia
STREET ADDRESS:	823 Barcelona Drive
CITY:	San Jose
STATE:	CA

```
ZIP:                     95130
PHONE:                   298-8489
BIRTHDAY:                8/23
MARITAL STATUS:          Single
DATE HIRED:              10/2/87
LAST RAISE:
PAY RATE:                4.00
TIME AVAILABLE:          Evenings
```

When you reach the last cell and all of the information is correct,

11. Press: (ENTER) to record the last field and **stay** on the same record.

Notice that the number of records (employees) in your file is displayed in the lower left corner of the screen.

Modifying a Form

Due to his need to quit school and get a full-time job, Raoul Villarreal resigned on December 18. In order to keep track of resignations and the reasons behind them, you decide to add two new fields.

To modify the design of the existing form, you will use the Design screen. Since you are already in the Form screen,

 1. Press: (ALT) to enter the Menu bar.

2. Type: **o** to choose the OPTIONS menu. Since the option you need, DEFINE FORM, is already highlighted,

3. Press: (ENTER)

The screen is very similar to the Form screen, but DESIGN appears in the Status bar at the bottom of the screen.

4. If the active cell is not the TIME AVAILABLE field, press (TAB) until it is.

5. Press: (→) to move the highlight to the end of the field.

6. Press: (→) **three times** to leave space between the TIME AVAILABLE and TERMINATION fields.

7. Type: **TERMINATION:** (don't forget the colon).

8. Press: (ENTER) to enter the new field into the form.

9. Press: (↓) **twice** to double space.

10. Press: (HOME) to move the highlight to the left margin.

┌ Active Field label will appear here

```
┌────────────────────────────────────────────────────────────────┐
│ ▐  Edit  Format  Window                                          │
│ LAST NAME: _____          FIRST NAME: _____             │
│ STREET ADDRESS: _____                          │
│ CITY: _____  STATE: _____ ZIP: _____       │
│ PHONE: _____                                               │
│ BIRTHDAY: _____                                            │
│ MARITAL STATUS: _____                                      │
│ DATE HIRED: _____                                          │
│ LAST RAISE: _____                               │
│ PAY RATE: _____                                           │
│ TIME AVAILABLE: _____  TERMINATION: _____             │
│ COMMENTS: _____                                       │
│                                                                │
│ Pg 1                    DESIGN                CL    PROFILE.WDB  │
│ Type field names. Press ALT to choose commands or F10 to exit Form Design. │
└────────────────────────────────────────────────────────────────┘
```

Figure 10-7

11. Type: **COMMENTS:** (Don't forget the colon.)

12. Press: (ENTER) to complete the form. Your screen should look something like Figure 10–7.

Notice that the space for comments is quite short. To allow more space for that field:

13. Move the highlight to the COMMENTS field.

14. Press: (ALT) to enter the Menu bar.

15. Type: **t** (for FORMAT menu).

16. Type: **w** to select the WIDTH option. When the WIDTH dialog box appears,

17. Type: **50** to change the width to 50 characters.

18. Press: (ENTER)

To exit the Design screen,

19. Press: (F10) to return to the Form screen.

Notice that the Status bar now displays the word FORM in the Status bar at the bottom of the screen.

Searching the Database Using a Form Screen ⃕

To find Raoul's record:

1. Press: **arrow** keys to move to the LAST NAME field.

2. Press: (ALT) to enter the Menu bar.

3. Type: **s** to choose the SELECT menu.

4. Type: **s** to select the SEARCH option. The SEARCH dialog box shown in Figure 10–8 appears.

Figure 10-8

5. Type: **Villarreal** in the "Search For:" field. Double check your spelling and capitalization. Since the rest of the dialog box is acceptable and <OK> is highlighted,

6. Press: (ENTER)

When Raoul's record appears:

7. Press: **arrow** keys to move the highlight to the TERMINATION field.

8. Type: **12/18/87**

9. Press: (TAB) to enter the date and move to the COMMENTS field

10. Type: **Needed full-time job.**

11. Press: (ENTER)

Sorting the Database File

Works can sort a file in either ascending (1, 2, 3,... or A, B, C, ...) or descending order, based upon one to three sort fields. Since you added a new employee, your file should be alphabetized again. First, return to the List view. If you have forgotten how:

1. Press: (ALT)

2. Type: **o** (the letter "o" for the OPTIONS menu).

3. Type: **v** to select the VIEW LIST option.

If the LAST NAME column is not highlighted:

4. Press: (CTRL)-(HOME) (hold down (CTRL), press (HOME), then release both keys) to return the cursor to the first column.

Select the first column. If you have forgotten how:

5. Press: (SHIFT)-(F8) (Hold down (SHIFT), press (F8), then release both.)

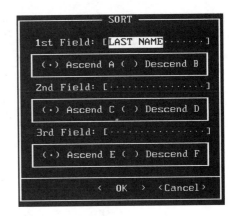

To sort columns:

6. Press: (ALT) to enter the Menu bar.

7. Type: **q** to choose the QUERY menu.

8. Type: **s** to select the SORT option. The SORT dialog box appears, as in Figure 10–9.

Since the program default assumes that you want to sort on the selected LAST NAME field in ascending order, and since that is the action desired,

9. Press: (ENTER) The list will reappear in proper order and alphabetized by last name.

Saving a File

Since you've made changes in the file, it's important that you save the altered file.

1. Press: (ALT) to enter the Menu bar. Since FILE is already highlighted,

2. Press: (ENTER) The FILE menu will drop down.

3. Type: **a** to select the SAVE AS option.

4. Type: **Profile2** to save the revised file under a new name.

5. Press: (ENTER) The red light will glow on the floppy disk drive as the file is being saved.

Review

If time permits, load *PROFILE.WDB* again and try to make the corrections without looking at the directions.

Summary

Congratulations! You have learned some basic database terms (such as files, records, fields, and query) and performed basic database functions (such as searching, sorting, adding fields to records, and adding records to a file).

Quitting *Works*

Follow this procedure to quit *Works:*

▶ 1. Press: (ALT) to enter the Menu bar. Since FILE is already highlighted,

2 Press: (ENTER)

3 Type: **x** to exit.

4. Type: **cd** to change the Current Directory to the root (main) directory from which you started.

5. **Take your disk out of Drive A and place it in the protective envelope.**

6. **Turn off the computer.**

Database: Worksheet 2

Setting the Scene

Remember the letter you composed to send to Birthday Club members in Chapter 4? In this chapter, you will create a simple database of Birthday Club members so each month hereafter the program can be directed to identify the members who should receive the letter.

In completing this chapter, you will:

- Create a simple database
- Design the form
- Add records
- Sort records
- Perform alphabetic and numeric searches
- Save the file for later use in integration
- Print the file

Starting *Works* ‖⇒

Figure 11-1

1. Type: **cd\works**

2. Press: (ENTER)

3. Type: **works**

4. Press: (ENTER)

The NEW menu appears, as in Figure 11–1.

Creating a New File

To create a new file, you must first designate the type of file desired. From the NEW menu:

‖⇒ 1. Press: ⬇ until Database is selected.

Since NEW is already selected,

2. Press: (ENTER) to display a blank design form as shown in Figure 11–2 (DESIGN displays in the Status bar at the bottom of the screen).

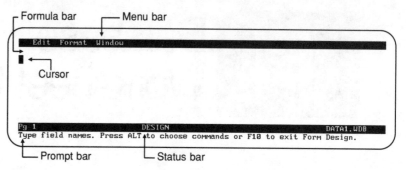

Figure 11-2

Creating the Form

The cursor (the illuminated rectangle near the the top of the screen) represents the point at which any typing will appear. If you want the first field to appear elsewhere, use the arrow keys to move the cursor. As you type, the keystrokes will appear in the Formula bar located immediately below the Menu bar. Use the backspace to correct any errors you might make.

A blank registration form which has been filled out by all Birthday Club members follows.

```
Last Name: _____    First Name: _____
Street Address: _____
City: _____    State: _____    Zip: _____
B/Month: _____
```

Figure 11-3

Use the skills you have learned to type the above form into the Design screen. Be sure to type the colons (:), but *do not* type the lines. When *Works* finds a colon, it interprets that as the end of one field, provides a line for later data input, and gets ready for instructions for another field.

If you have problems beginning your form, you may follow the directions below:

1. Type: **Last Name:** (This is the name of the first field in your form.) Don't forget the colon!

2. Press: (ENTER) to enter the first field. Your screen should look like Figure 11–4.

Notice that the first field in the form is highlighted and that what you typed is displayed in the Formula bar. When you use the (→) to move the highlight, the printing in the Formula bar disappears because the active cell will then be in a blank

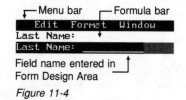

Figure 11-4

portion of the form. The program added an underline after the name of the field. Don't worry about the length of the line; you will expand the size of the field later.

3. Press: $\rightarrow$ until the cursor is horizontally in the middle of the screen, in position to type the next field name.

4. Type: **First Name:** (remember that colon).

5. Press: $\downarrow$ to enter the field *and* move down to the next line for the next field.

To move the cursor to the beginning of the line and enter the street address field name:

6. Press: (HOME) to move the cursor to the beginning of the current line.

7. Type: **Street Address:**

8. Press: $\downarrow$

Think you can type the rest yourself? Give it a try! If you need help, refer to the instructions that follow. When you finish, go on to the heading **Changing the Size of Fields.**

9. Type: **City:**

10. Press: $\rightarrow$ **several times** until the cursor is in the middle of the line of typing.

11. Type: **State:**

12. Press: $\rightarrow$ **twice**

13. Type: **ZIP:**

14. Press: $\downarrow$

15. Press: (HOME)

16. Type: **B/Month:** as an abbreviation for the birth month.

17. Press: (ENTER)

If you discover mistakes *after* they have been entered, move the cursor to that field and retype.

Changing the Size of Fields

The State and Zip fields are of ample size, but some of the other fields should be changed to allow for different size entries. To change the size of the B/Month field and field name to a total of 15 characters,

1. **Move the cursor to the B/Month: field.**

2. Press: (ALT) to enter the Menu bar.

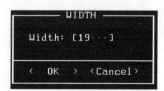

Figure 11-5

3. Type: **t** to choose the FORMAT menu.

4. Type: **w** to select the WIDTH option. The WIDTH Option dialog box shown in Figure 11–5 will appear.

5. Type: **15** to replace the default of 19 spaces.

6. Press: (ENTER)

Repeat steps 1-6 above to change the size of the City, Street Address, Last Name, and First Name fields as follows:

Field name	Size
City	20
Street Address	40
Last Name	30
First Name	30

To exit the Design screen,

7. Press: (F10)

A blank form will appear on the screen. Notice that the Status bar now displays the word FORM at the bottom of the screen.

Entering New Data

Chris Hughes has given you a stack of membership cards that need to be recorded. You will test your database by first entering the data about a few members, then sorting and querying the database.

Record the Club members listed in Figure 11-6 into your newly created database. If you need help, follow the directions given below. If you do not need help, turn to the heading **"Sorting the File"** after recording the membership cards shown in Figure 11–6.

Notice that when the month is entered, it is treated as a numeric, not alpha, field. *Works* abbreviates months and aligns them, as it does all values, on the right.

 1. Use the arrow keys to move to the Last Name field.

2. Type: **McNamara**

3. Press: (TAB) to enter and move to the First Name field.

4. Type: **Jane**

5. Press: (TAB) to enter and move to the Street Address field.

6. Type: **719 Morse St.**

7. Press: (TAB) to enter and move to the City field.

Last Name: McNamara	First Name: Jane
Street Address: 719 Morse St.	
City: San Jose	State: CA Zip: 95128
B/Month: February	

Last Name: Kline	First Name: Calvin
Street Address: 721 St. John St.	
City: San Jose	State: CA Zip: 95130
B/Month: May	

Last Name: Boyle	First Name: Lance
Street Address: 7415 Forest Ave.	
City: San Jose	State: CA Zip: 95128
B/Month: January	

Last Name: Pang	First Name: Alice
Street Address: 721 Saratoga Ave.	
City: Saratoga	State: CA Zip: 95070
B/Month: September	

Last Name: Montague	First Name: Charles
Street Address: 73715 Bascom Ave.	
City: Los Gatos	State: CA Zip: 95030
B/Month: January	

Last Name: Sakamoto	First Name: Sachi
Street Address: 87 Rocky Lane	
City: San Jose	State: CA Zip: 95130
B/Month: August	

Last Name: Wong	First Name: Mohammed
Street Address: 7711 Campbell Ave.	
City: Campbell	State: CA Zip: 95008
B/Month: March	

Last Name: Mock	First Name: Cherry
Street Address: 666 Esmeralda Ct.	
City: Campbell	State: CA Zip: 95008
B/Month: April	

Last Name: Piccolo	First Name: Sal
Street Address: 7988 Latimer Ave.	
City: San Jose	State: CA Zip: 95117
B/Month: January	

Last Name: Zachary	First Name: Scot
Street Address: 7104 DeAnza Blvd.	
City: Cupertino	State: CA Zip: 95014
B/Month: November	

Figure 11-6

8. Type: **San Jose**

9. Press: (TAB) to enter and move to the State field.

10. Type: **CA**

11. Press: (TAB) to enter and move to the ZIP field.

12. Type: **95128**

13. Press: (TAB) to enter and move to the Birth Month field.

14. Type: **February** (*Works* displays the month using a three-letter abbreviation form).

15. Press: (TAB)

Notice that pressing (TAB) this last time moved you to the next record. (See the number 2 displayed in the lower left corner in the Status bar? That indicates that you are in the second record in this file.) If you want to be sure that you made no mistakes in the first record,

16. Press: (CTRL)-(PGUP)

The Status bar at the bottom contains directions on how to get to the previous and next records in case you forget. To get to the next blank form,

17. Press: (CTRL)-(PGDN)

Repeat steps 1–15 in the previous section to enter the data for the other members of the club.

Sorting the File

One of the many benefits of a database program is that it will perform all kinds of sorts for you. For example, you can sort by ZIP code for mailing purposes, or by birthdate for your birthday letters, or by address to see if an extraordinarily high number are registered from any one address. When you get all of your Birthday Club members entered, you will probably want to alphabetize the list to be sure that no one person will be getting more than one letter.

First, return to the List view. If you need a review:

1. Press: (ALT)

2. Type: **o** (the letter "o" for the OPTIONS menu).

3. Type: **v** to select the VIEW LIST option.

4. **The cursor should be in the upper left corner of the screen.** If it is not, follow step a below; otherwise, go on to step 5.

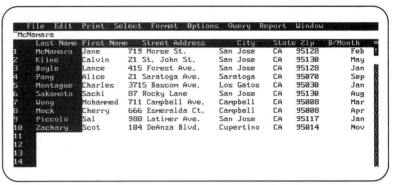

Figure 11-7

a. Press: (CTRL)-(HOME) to return to the upper left corner of the screen.

5. Press (SHIFT)-(F8), to select the entire first column. Your screen should look similar to Figure 11–7.

To sort columns,

6. Press: (ALT) to enter the Menu bar.

7. Type: **q** to choose the QUERY menu.

8. Type: **s** to select the SORT option. The SORT dialog box shown in Figure 11–8 appears.

The program has correctly guessed that you want to sort on the Last Name field in ascending order; but if ten people have the same last name, you also want *Works* to sort those ten by first name.

9. Press: (TAB) until the cursor is in the box labeled 2nd Field:

10. Type: **First Name**

Since the rest of the dialog box is correct and <OK> is highlighted,

11. Press: (ENTER)

The database is now in alphabetical order by last and first name.

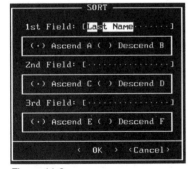

Figure 11-8

Querying the Database

You should still be in the List view; if you are not, follow the steps in the previous section to return to the List view.

You are now ready to instruct *Works* to display the names and addresses of only those customers who have birthdays in January. Do you remember how? If you need help,

1. Press: (ALT) to enter the Menu bar.

2. Type: **q** to choose the QUERY menu. Since DEFINE is already highlighted,

3. Press: (ENTER) to select the DEFINE option.

A blank form screen appears with QUERY displayed in the Status bar at the bottom of the screen. You will use this screen to define your query.

4. Press: (TAB) until the highlight reaches the B/Month field.

5. Type: **January**   Because of the way *Works* handles data and depending upon which IBM model you are using, January will be abbreviated to 1/1/80 or Jan.

6. Press: (ENTER) to record the query criteria.

7. Press: (F10) to exit the QUERY screen and activate the query.

A list of those Club members with January birthdays will be displayed.

To clear the QUERY definition,

1. Press: (ALT) to enter the Menu bar.

2. Type: **q** (the QUERY menu). Since DEFINE is highlighted,

3. Press: (ENTER) to display the DEFINE form. To remove the QUERY criteria,

4. Press: (TAB) enough times to move the highlight to the Birth Month field.

5. Press: (ALT) to enter the Menu bar. Since EDIT is already highlighted in this abbreviated menu,

6. Press: (ENTER)   The EDIT menu will drop down.

7. Type: **e** to select the CLEAR option. A blank QUERY screen displays (see Status bar at the bottom).

8. Press: (F10) as directed at the bottom of the screen to exit QUERY.

Saving a File

Since this is a new file, it's important that you save it.

1. **Look at the Status bar.** *Works* automatically assigns a default file name to your file. In this case the default file name is *DATA1.WDB*. The file extension ".WDB" tells you that this is a database file. However, the file name *Data1* is

not very descriptive, so you will save the file using another, more descriptive file name.

2. Press: (ALT) to enter the Menu bar.

3. Press: (ENTER) The FILE menu will drop down.

4. Type: **a** to select SAVE AS....

5. **Look at the Current Drive line**. (It's the second line in the dialog box.)

6. **If the Current Drive is *not* A:** follow steps a through c; otherwise, continue to step 7.

   a. Press: (TAB) until you reach the Other Drives & Directories box.

   b. Press: (↓) until [-A-] is highlighted.

   c. Press: (ENTER) The red light on Drive A: will glow briefly and the cursor will return to the File Name line.

7. Type: **Members**

8. Press: (ENTER) The red light will glow on the floppy disk drive as the file is being saved.

Printing a File

Turn on your printer and check that it is ready to print.

1. Press: (ALT) to enter the Menu bar.

2. Type: **p** to select the PRINT menu.

3. Press: **L** to select LAYOUT.

4. Press: (TAB) to move the cursor to the LEFT MARGIN line.

5. Type: **0** (the number 0).

6. Press: (TAB) to move the cursor to the RIGHT MARGIN line.

7. Type: **0** (the number).

8. Press: (ENTER)

9. Press: (ALT) to enter the Menu bar.

10. Type: **p** to select the PRINT menu.

11. Press: (ENTER) The PRINT dialog box will appear.

12. Press: (ENTER) One copy will be printed.

Review

If time permits, try to create another database without looking at these directions.

Summary

Congratulations! You have practiced some basic database operations such as creating a file, sorting, and querying. You have learned that database is a very complex, powerful application.

Quitting *Works*

1. Press: (ALT) to enter the Menu bar. Since FILE is already highlighted,

2. Press: (ENTER)

3. Type: **x** to exit.

4. **Take your disk out of Drive A and place it in the protective envelope.**

5. **Turn the computer off.**

12 Database: Worksheet 3

It is the beginning of a hot summer weekend and one of your employees calls in sick. You need a replacement who can work the same hours. What do you do? The database you have stored on your computer contains the needed data about all of your employees; however, you have now identified a need to work with a subset of the data to fill a particular need — to locate all employees available to work at a particular hour. In this chapter, you will produce a simple, easy-to-read database report containing the names of each employee listed according to hours of availability and including phone numbers. Only the required data will be extracted from the database to create the report. Much of the actual data in the database will not appear in the report. In completing this chapter, you will:

- Create a simple report
- Select fields for the report
- Sort records in the report
- Add titles to a report
- Format a report
- Print the report

The finished report is shown in Figure 12–1.

```
                        EMPLOYEE ROSTER
                        Time Available


        LAST NAME       FIRST NAME     PHONE          TIME AVAILABLE

        Carrillo        Angela         291-8654       Afternoons
        Jacobsen        Russ           378-1330       Afternoons
        Prada           Josephine      867-1779       Afternoons
        Tyler           Geoffrey       299-4151       Afternoons

        Carlson         Roberta        255-6100       Evenings
        Villarreal      Raoul          289-4050       Evenings
        Yee             Wendy          867-4891       Evenings

        Mansur          Gloria         353-4454       Mornings
        Williams        Corinne        379-1008       Mornings
```

Figure 12-1

Starting *Works*

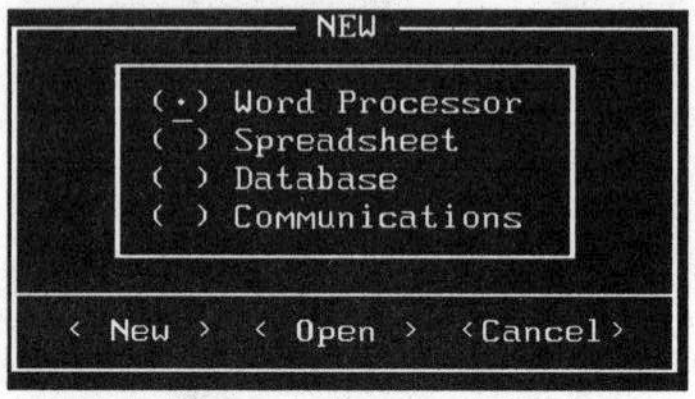
NEW
(·) Word Processor
( ) Spreadsheet
( ) Database
( ) Communications
< New > < Open > <Cancel>

Figure 12-2

1. Type: **cd\works**
2. Press: (ENTER)
3. Type: **works**
4. Press: (ENTER)

The screen will resemble Figure 12–2.

Opening a File

A database file has already been prepared for you. The file is stored on your data disk under the file name *PROFILE.WDB* .

1. Press: (TAB) key to move the cursor selection to <OPEN>.
2. Press: (ENTER) The OPEN dialog box will appear. (See Figure 12–3.)
3. Press: (TAB) until the cursor reaches the Other Drives box.
4. Press: (↓) until [-A-] is highlighted.
5. **Insert your data disk in Drive A.**
6. Press: (ENTER) A list of file names will appear in the left-hand box. If *PROFILE.WDB* is among the files listed, skip to step 11. If *PROFILE.WDB* is not listed,
7. Press: (TAB) until the cursor moves to the right-hand box.
8. Press: (↓) until the cursor moves to the Database line.
9. Press: (ENTER) Only database files (.WDB) should now be displayed in the left-hand box. Your screen should be similar to Figure 12–4.
10. Press: (TAB) to move the cursor to the left-hand box.

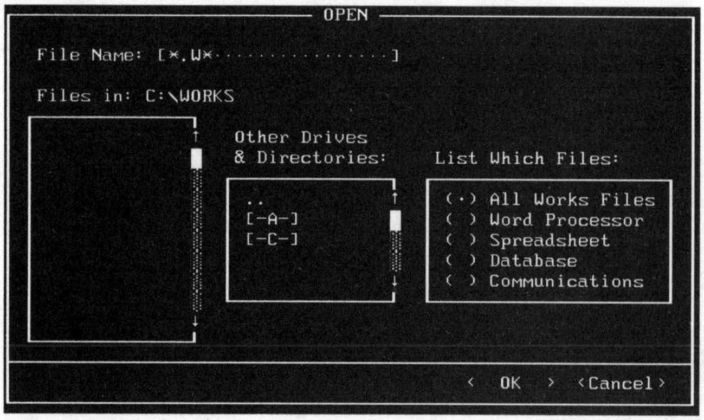
OPEN
File Name: [*.W*...............]
Files in: C:\WORKS
Other Drives
& Directories:
List Which Files:
..
[-A-]
[-C-]
(·) All Works Files
( ) Word Processor
( ) Spreadsheet
( ) Database
( ) Communications
< OK > <Cancel>

Figure 12-3

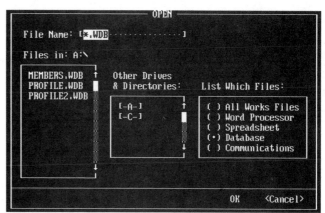

Figure 12-4

11. Press: (↓) until the file name *PROFILE.WDB* becomes highlighted.

12. Press: (ENTER) The *PROFILE.WDB* file will appear on the screen.

Producing a report from a database in *Works* can be accomplished in one of two ways:

1. Creating a report from scratch.

2. Creating a report using *Works'* speed-reporting facility.

You will be using the speed-reporting method to create an Employee Roster report from the *Profile* database. You will then modify the report to improve its appearance.

Deleting Unwanted Fields from the Report

The first step in creating the report is to remove all unwanted fields from the database. Since you want a report showing your employees, their phone numbers, and the times they are available to work, you must delete all the other fields for the purpose of this report. As you are deleting fields, remember that you are simply deleting them from the report you are creating; you are *not* deleting them from the database itself.

1. Move the cursor to the STREET ADDRESS column.

2. Press: (F8) to extend the highlight to adjoining columns.

3. Press: (→) until four columns, up to and including the ZIP column, are highlighted.

4. Press: (ALT) to enter the Menu bar.

5. Type: **s** (to choose the SELECT menu).

6. Type: **f** (to select the FIELD option). All four columns are now highlighted.

7. Press: (ALT) to enter the Menu bar.

8. Type: **e** to choose the EDIT menu.

9. Type: **d** to select the DELETE option.

The highlighted columns are removed from the screen, and the remaining columns have moved to fill in the vacated space.

Since the phone number column is needed for your report, you will skip that column. You will now remove the Birthday column and the four columns that follow it:

10. Press: (→) to move the highlight to the Birthday column.

11. Press: (F8) to extend the highlight to other columns to be deleted.

12. Press: (→) until the Pay Rate column is highlighted. The Pay Rate column may not be displayed on the screen, but it will appear as you scroll to the right using the (→).

13. Press: (ALT) to enter the Menu bar.

14. Type: **s** to choose the SELECT menu.

15. Type: **f** to select the FIELD option. The columns to be deleted will be highlighted.

16. Press: (ALT) to enter the Menu bar.

17. Type: **e** (EDIT menu).

18. Type: **d** (DELETE option). (Note that the columns have been removed from the screen.)

To return to Column A and display the data remaining in the report,

19. Press: (HOME)

Sorting Fields in a Report

Your screen should now look something like Figure 12–5.

In order to make it easier to find employees able to work at specific times of the day, you will sort the remaining data by the TIME AVAILABLE field:

1. Press: (ALT) to enter the Menu bar.

2. Type: **q** to choose the QUERY menu.

3. Type: **s** to select the SORT option. The SORT dialog box appears as shown in Figure 12–6.

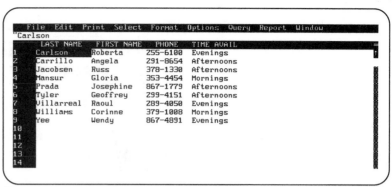

Figure 12-5

The program has incorrectly assumed that you want to sort on the LAST NAME field in ascending order. To change the name of the highlighted sort field,

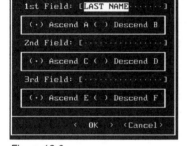

Figure 12-6

4. Type: **TIME AVAILABLE**   That title will appear as the first sort field.

Since the rest of the dialog box is correct and <OK> is highlighted,

5. Press: (ENTER)

Because the database records are now sorted alphabetically on the TIME AVAILABLE field:

a. Employees available in the Afternoons appear first.

b. Employees available in the Evenings appear second.

c. Employees available in the Mornings appear last.

Changing Column Width

The report would look much better if all the columns were wider.

1. Move the cursor highlight to the upper left-hand corner of the screen. The name Carlson should be highlighted.

2. Press: (F8) to extend the highlight.

3. Press: (CTRL)-(END) to select the entire report.

4. Press: (ALT) to enter the Menu bar.

5. Type: **t** (FORMAT menu).

6. Type: **w** (WIDTH option).

7. Type: **15** as the new column width.

The Body of the Report will consist of data taken from these fields of the database.

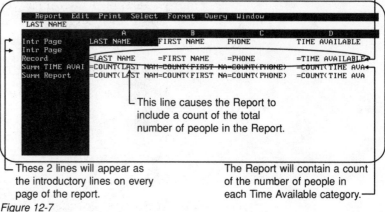

This line causes the Report to include a count of the total number of people in the Report.

These 2 lines will appear as the introductory lines on every page of the report.

The Report will contain a count of the number of people in each Time Available category.

Figure 12-7

8. Press: (ENTER) All the columns are now 15 spaces wide.

Creating the Report

Works simplifies the creation of simple reports through its speed-reporting method. To see how speed reporting works,

1. Press: (ALT) to enter the Menu bar.

2. Type: **r** to choose the REPORT menu.

3. Type: **n** to select the NEW option. The report screen appears as in Figure 12–7.

4. Press: (ALT) to enter the Menu bar. Since the option you desire, REPORT, is already highlighted,

5. Press: (ENTER) to display the REPORT menu.

6. Type: **v** to select the VIEW option. Your screen should look like Figure 12–8.

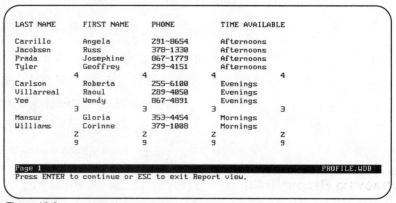

Figure 12-8

Adding Headings

Your report now has all the data needed, but it would be much more effective if headings were added to identify the purpose of the report and to label specific items and column headings.

▐▶ 1. Press: (ESC) to return to the Report screen.

To insert a few lines for a title and subtitles,

2. **Move the cursor to the top of LAST NAME column.**

3. Press: (ALT) to enter the Menu bar.

4. Type: **s** to choose the SELECT menu. Since ROW is already selected,

5. Press: (ENTER)

6. Press: (F8) to extend the highlight.

7. Press: (↓) three times to highlight the lines needed for the titles.

8. Press: (ALT) to enter the Menu bar.

9. Type: **e** (EDIT menu).

10. Type: **i** (INSERT option). The INSERT dialog box appears.

11. Press: (↑) until INTR REPORT is highlighted. (Think of INTR REPORT as being *intr*oductory lines of a *report*).

12. Press: (ENTER)

The screen now displays four Intr Report rows on your report screen with the cursor on the first Intr Report row. Since the title of the report would look better if it began toward the center of the page,

13. Press: (→) to move to Column B.

14. Press: **space bar five times** so the heading will be closer to the center of the page.

15. Type: **EMPLOYEE ROSTER**

16. Press: (↓) to enter the main title *and* move down one line, in position to type a subtitle.

17. Press: **space bar five times.**

18. Type: **TIMES AVAILABLE**

19. Press: (↓) The heading lines are complete.

Removing Record Totals

You should still be in the Report screen. Although the lines showing the total number of employees available to work during each shift and the total number of employees included in the report might be valuable for some reports, they are very distracting here. The report would look much better without them. To eliminate both summary lines from your report,

1. **Move the cursor to "Summ TIME AVAIL" row.**

2. Press: (ALT) to enter the Menu bar.

3. Type: **s** (SELECT menu) Since the ROW option is already highlighted,

4. Press: (ENTER)

5. Press: (F8) to extend the selection.

6. Press: (↓) until Summ Report is highlighted.

7. Press: (ALT) to enter the Menu bar.

8. Type: **e** (EDIT menu).

9. Type: **e** (CLEAR option). DELETE will *eliminate* the present line; CLEAR will *erase the content* of the line, but leave a blank line between each time category.

Viewing the Modified Report

To view your modified report,

1. Press: (ALT) to enter the Menu bar. REPORT is highlighted.

2. Press: (ENTER) to display the REPORT menu.

3. Type: **v** to VIEW option. Your screen should look something like Figure 12–9.

To return to the report screen,

4. Press: (ESC)

```
                     EMPLOYEE ROSTER
                      Time Available

    LAST NAME       FIRST NAME      PHONE          TIME AVAILABLE

    Carrillo        Angela          291-8654       Afternoons
    Jacobsen        Russ            378-1330       Afternoons
    Prada           Josephine       867-1779       Afternoons
    Tyler           Geoffrey        299-4151       Afternoons

    Carlson         Roberta         255-6100       Evenings
    Villarreal      Raoul           289-4050       Evenings
    Yee             Wendy           867-4891       Evenings

    Mansur          Gloria          353-4454       Mornings
    Williams        Corinne         379-1008       Mornings
    Page 1                                                    PROFILE.WDB
    Press ENTER to continue or ESC to exit Report view.
```

Figure 12-9

Printing a Report

To print the list of employees and their available times, follow the steps in this section. You should still be in the Report screen. Check to see that the printer is on and the paper is properly positioned.

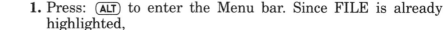

1. Press: (ALT) to enter the Menu bar.
2. Type: **p** (PRINT menu). Since PRINT is already highlighted,
3. Press: (ENTER) The PRINT dialog box appears.
4. Press: (ENTER) to accept all the default settings displayed.

Printing should begin in a few seconds. Your printout should be similar to that displayed in Figure 12-1.

5. Press: (F10) to exit Report screen.

Review

If time permits, try to create another report without looking at these directions.

Summary

Congratulations! You should now be able to prepare special purpose reports using one database. You have already used many of the tools you need to begin exploring the specifics of that powerful function.

Quitting *Works*

1. Press: (ALT) to enter the Menu bar. Since FILE is already highlighted,
2. Press: (ENTER)
3. Type: **x** to exit. A dialog box appears asking whether the changes made should be saved. The changes you made were only for the purpose of creating this special report. Therefore, you do not want to save them. To retain the database in its original state,
4. Press: (TAB) until <NO> is highlighted.
5. Press: (ENTER)
6. **Take your disk out of Drive A and place it in the protective envelope.**
7. **Turn the computer off.**

13 Database Shortcuts and Other Features

Setting the Scene

Now that you have used your employee database, you probably have thought of modifications which you would have made had *you* designed it. Use the directions that follow to make the file more meaningful, or design a completely different database if you wish. In this chapter you will

- Learn some keyboard shortcuts for the database tool
- Use the COPY command
- Learn about calculated fields

As was true in the final word processing and spreadsheet chapters, this section requires more imagination to complete. See how many of the features you can incorporate into one project — that's the best way to learn!

Database Shortcuts

Following are shortcuts for some of the most commonly used functions in database operations. This is not a complete list. Consult the *Microsoft Works Reference* manual for further information.

Selection Shortcut

To select	Press these keys
Row	(CTRL)-(F8)
Column	(SHIFT)-(F8)
Entire DataBase	(CTRL)-(SHIFT)-(F8)

Other Shortcuts

To do this	Press these keys	Available from
Go to Another Record or Field	(F5)	Form and List views
Go to Beginning	(CTRL)-(HOME)	Form and List views
Go to End	(CTRL)-(END)	Form and List views (moves to first blank form in Form view)

Go to Next Record	(CTRL)-(PGUP) or (CTRL)-(PGDN)	Form view
Switch View	(F9)	Form and List views
Copy	(SHIFT)-(F3)	*Form view:* copies selected record to another record *List view:* copies selected cell(s) to other cells or other *Works* files
Move	(F3)	*Form view:* moves entire record to a new location *List view:* moves selected rows or columns to new locations; entire row(s) or column(s) must be selected *Design view:* moves selected field to new location
Edit	(F2)	Puts blinking cursor on Formula bar; backspace to delete character(s), type in correction

Changing a Form Using the Design Screen

To Display Design Screen	1. Open file. 2. On Form screen, choose OPTIONS menu. 3. Select DEFINE FORM option.
To Move a Cell/Cells	1. Select field. 2. Choose EDIT menu, MOVE option. 3. Move cursor to new location. 4. Press (ENTER)
To Change Name or Label	1. Select field or label. 2. Press (F2) (cursor in Formula bar). 3. Correct field name or label. 4. Press (ENTER)
To Add a Field	1. Move cursor to desired location. 2. Type field name, followed by a colon. 3. Press (ENTER)

To Delete a Field	1. Select field to be deleted.
	2. Choose EDIT menu, DELETE option.
	3. Press (ENTER)

Using the Copy Command

The copy command works differently in each screen:

List Screen:	Copies selected fields to another part of the database. You can also copy to other *Works* files.
Form Screen:	Copies selected record to another record.
Design Screen:	Copies selected field name to a new location.

Using Calculated Fields

Entering data into a database is not limited to simple text or numbers. You can also enter formulas or equations which reference other fields in the record. A field containing a formula is referred to as a calculated field. A field may contain a function like those used in spreadsheets (for example, SUM, AVG, and so on).

Look, for example, at the Figure 13–1. The Active Cell **E2** shows an equation in the Formula bar; but the cell itself displays the result of that formula, which contains references to two other fields in the record (that is, No. and Cost). The asterisk, "$*$" means, "to multiply."

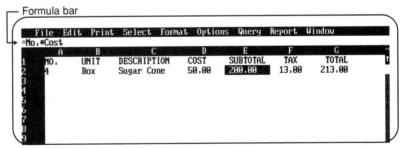

Figure 13-1

As you can see, there are many possibilities to using a database. For more information you may want to use the HELP or TUTORIAL features. Indices for these features are available in the WINDOW menu.

14 Integration

Introduction

Many computer users sometimes have a need to combine the capabilities of one productivity software tool with those of another. If a person uses *separate* word processor, spreadsheet, database, charting, or other kinds of programs, it can be difficult to combine the output from each of them. With an integrated program such as *Microsoft Works*, it is easy to develop a combined report that uses material generated by each of the tools available in *Works*. This chapter gives you detailed instructions about how to use the word processor, spreadsheet, and database tools to create one document which includes material from each of the *Works* tools.

Setting the Scene

Remember the letter you composed earlier, inviting Birthday Club members to come in for a free ice cream cone in the month of their birthday? Now it's time to personalize those letters and print them out. You will merge each letter with information taken from the Club member database you created earlier. Figure 14–1 shows you the different parts of the finished product.

You will also use the word processor to write a memo to the owner presenting the sales figures for last week. That memo will include material taken from a spreadsheet file.

In completing this chapter, you will:

- Prepare a word processing document for merging with a database
- Prepare a word processing document containing a printout of a spreadsheet
- Work with more than one document at a time in memory
- Print merged documents

Starting *Works*   ‖⇒

1. Type: **cd\works**
2. Press: (ENTER)
3. Type: **works**

```
 File  Edit  Print  Select  Format  Options  Window
[ · · · · · · · · 1 · · · · · · · · 2 · · · · · · · · 3 · · · · · · · · 4 · · · · · · · · 5 · · · · · · · ] · · ·
»December 20, 1987




Dear Birthday Club Member:

HAPPY BIRTHDAY!

To help celebrate your special day next month, we are
enclosing 2 coupons that can be exchanged for free ice cream
cones in any of our delicious flavors.

Our flavor of the month is Banana Pecan, but of course you
may choose from any of our traditional flavors.

We are looking forward to seeing you next month!
```

Text is taken from the Word
Processing document.

```
 LAST NAME    FIRST NAME    STREET ADDRESS      CITY       STATE   ZIP
Carlson      Roberta       575 Pebble Beach Dr. Cupertino   CA     95014
Carrillo     Angela        863 Columbia Dr.    San Jose    CA     95130
Jacobsen     Russ          283 Campbell Avenue Campbell    CA     95008
Mansur       Gloria        164 Blossom Hill Road Los Gatos CA     95030
Prada        Josephine     675 Big Basin Way   Saratoga    CA     95070
Tyler        Geoffrey      1001 No. Bascom Ave. San Jose   CA     95128
Villarreal   Raoul         3065 Maui Drive     San Jose    CA     95130
Williams     Corinne       248 Budd Avenue     Campbell    CA     95008
Yee          Wendy         1864 McFarland Ave. Saratoga    CA     95070
```

Names and addresses are taken
from the Database document.

```
 File  Edit  Print  Select  Format  Options  Window
[ · · · · · · · · 1 · · · · · · · · 2 · · · · · · · · 3 · · · · · · · · 4 · · · · · · · · 5 · · · · · · · ] · · ·
»December 20, 1987

Roberta Carlson
575 Pebble Beach Dr.
Cupertino, CA 95014

Dear Birthday Club Member:

HAPPY BIRTHDAY!

To help celebrate your special day next month, we are
enclosing 2 coupons that can be exchanged for free ice cream
cones in any of our delicious flavors.

Our flavor of the month is Banana Pecan, but of course you
may choose from any of our traditional flavors.
```

The new document
contains parts from
each of the old
documents.

Figure 14-1

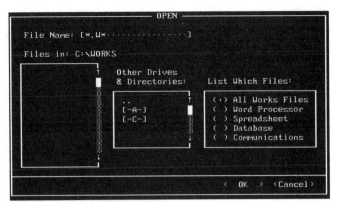

Figure 14-2

Opening the Database

Using *Works'* ability to use both the database tool and the word processing tool at the same time, you will print the birthday letter again (but this time with the name and address of each person with January birthdays incorporated into each letter).

So that *Works* will have the membership records available for use in memory, first open the file, *MEMBERS.WDB.*

1. Press: (TAB) key until <OPEN> option chosen.

2. Press: (ENTER) The OPEN dialog box will appear. (See Figure 14–2.)

3. Press: (TAB) until cursor moves to the middle box.

4. Press: (↓) until [-A-] becomes highlighted.

5. **Insert your data disk in Drive A.**

6. Press: (ENTER) A list of file names will appear in the left-hand box.

7. Press: (TAB) until cursor moves to the right-hand box.

8. Press: (↓) until "Database" is highlighted.

9. Press: (ENTER) Your screen should look somewhat like Figure 14–3.

10. Press: (TAB) until cursor moves to the left-hand box.

11. Press: (↓) until the file name *MEMBERS.WDB* becomes highlighted.

12. Press: (ENTER) The *Members* file will appear on the screen.

Opening the Word Processing File

The form letter to Birthday Club members is on your data disk under the file name, *B-DAY.WPS.* To open that file,

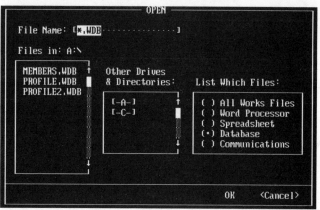

Figure 14-3

1. Press: (ALT) to enter the Menu bar. Since FILE is already highlighted,

2. Press: (ENTER) to drop down the FILE Menu.

3. Type: **o** (the letter "o") to select OPEN option.

4. Press: (TAB) until marker reaches the LIST WHICH FILES block.

5. Press: ↓ to highlight Word Processor.

6. Press: (ENTER)   The left-hand box containing the list of files will now only show files with an extension of .WPS.

7. Press: (TAB) until cursor moves to the file list block.

8. Press: ↓ until *B-DAY.WPS* is highlighted.

9. Press: (ENTER)   The Birthday Club letter will appear on your screen.

Viewing the Open Documents

Figure 14-4

Works allows you to have up to eight documents open at one time. To see the names of the open files and to activate a file,

1. Press: (ALT) to enter the Menu bar.

2. Type: **w** to choose the WINDOW menu. (See Figure 14–4.)

The bottom block displays the files that are currently open. To work directly with the *Members* database file,

3. Type: **1** (the number 1) since that is the number next to the *Members* file. To return to the *Birthday* (*B-day*) word processing file,

4. Press: (ALT) to enter the Menu bar.

5. Type: **w** (WINDOW menu).

6. Type: **2** (the number for the *B-day* file).

Preparing to Merge

In order to personalize the letter, you will add the recipient's name and address four lines below the date, two lines above the present greeting, "Dear Birthday Club Member," as in Figure 14–5.

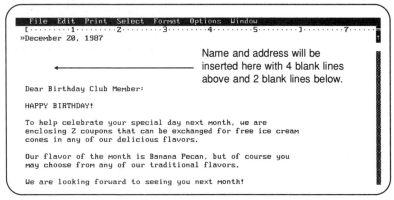

Figure 14-5

Inserting Placeholders

With the cursor in position at the beginning of the date line,

1. Press: ⓓ **four times**.

2. Press: (ALT) to enter the Menu bar.

3. Type: **e** (EDIT menu).

4. Type: **f** (INSERT FIELD). The INSERT FIELD dialog box will appear.

5. If necessary, press (TAB) to move the cursor to the Field Name field.

6. Type: **first name**   This is the name of the database field you need printed in this position.

7. Press: (ENTER) to enter the command. The dialog box disappears and you can see that <<first name>> has been inserted in your letter in the position where the first name of the recipient should go. The double angle brackets << and >> are called *placeholders* and are used to tell *Works* to insert data into the letter at the positions the placeholders appear. The data that will be inserted is obtained from the named field of the currently open database.

You must arrange the placeholders exactly where you want the real data to appear in the finished letter. Since a space should appear between the first and last name, a space is left between those two field name placeholders.

8. Press: **space bar** to insert the space between first and last names.

9. Press: (ALT) to enter the Menu bar.

10. Type: **e** (EDIT menu).

11. Type: **f** (INSERT FIELD). If necessary, press (TAB) to move cursor to Field Name field.

12. Type: **last name**   This is the name of the next field to be inserted.

13. Press: (ENTER) to complete the command. The letter appears again with <<last name>> included.

14. Press: (ENTER) again to move the cursor to the next line and in position to type the next field name. Since you are in the INSERT mode, notice that lines will be added whenever you press the (ENTER) key.

Use steps 9 through 14 as a guide for inserting placeholders for the remaining field names. The example that follows in Figure 14–6 may also help you. Remember to type a comma after the placeholder for City and leave a space between State and ZIP. When you are through, the screen should look something like Figure 14–6.

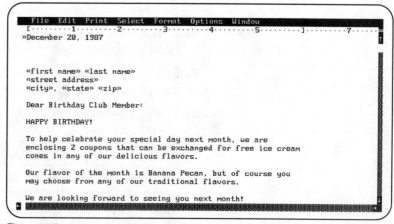

Figure 14-6

Changing the Greeting

To change the greeting to include the recipient's name rather than the impersonal "Dear Birthday Club Member",

1. **Use the arrow keys** to move the cursor to the "B" in Birthday Club Member.

2. Press: (F8) to extend the selection.

3. Press: (→) until "Birthday Club Member" is highlighted.

4. Press: (DEL) to erase the selected material.

5. Press: (ALT) to enter the Menu bar.

6. Type: **e** (EDIT menu).

7. Type: **f** (INSERT FIELD). If necessary, press (TAB) to move cursor to Field Name field.

8. Type: **first name**

9. Press: (ENTER) to complete the insert.

The line at the cursor's position should read: Dear <<first name>>:

Selecting the January Birthdays

You are now ready to print the letters. First, you must select only the records in the database for Birthday Club members who have a birthday in January.

1. Press: (ALT) to enter the Menu bar.

2. Type: **w** (WINDOW menu).

3. Type: **1** (the number identifying *MEMBERS.WDB* file).

4. Press: (ALT) to enter the Menu bar.

5. Type: **q** (QUERY menu). Since DEFINE is already selected,

6. Press: (ENTER)   A blank (or almost blank form) will appear.

7. Press: **arrow** keys until the highlight rests in the B/Month field.

8. Type: **January**

9. Press: (ENTER)   Note that *Works* displays the date in abbreviated form. Don't worry about it. The query will be successful anyway.

10. Press: (F10) to initiate the query. The *Members* file appears once again, but this time the only members who are shown are those with birthdays in January.

Returning to the Form Letter

Now you have to return to the Word Processing window to complete the print operation.

⇒
1. Press: (ALT) to enter the Menu bar.

2. Type: **w** (WINDOW menu).

3. Type: **2** (the number assigned to the *B-day* file).

Printing the Merged Document

Finally, to begin printing,

⇒
1. Press: (ALT) to enter the Menu bar.

2. Type: **p** (PRINT menu).

3. Type: **m** to select PRINT MERGE option. The PRINT MERGE dialog box in which all open database files are listed is displayed. (See Figure 14–7.)

4. Press: ⓙ until *MEMBERS.WDB* is highlighted. Since <OK> is already highlighted,

5. Press: (ENTER)   The PRINT dialog box appears. Since all the defaults are acceptable,

6. Press: (ENTER)

The letters will soon be printed.

Figure 14-7

More Scene Setting

In order to keep abreast of the profits of the business, Chris developed an income statement and asked you to make further changes in it. You are now ready to submit it to Chris for her approval. Because a brief introduction and explanation of the income statement would be desirable, you will use the word processing tool to create a memo as a part of the spreadsheet. (See Figure 14–8.)

Opening a New Word Processing Document

This section contains instructions that will help you to open a new word processing file and create the memo.

⇒
1. Press: (ALT) to enter the Menu bar. Since FILE is already highlighted,

2. Press: (ENTER)   Since NEW is already highlighted,

3. Press: (ENTER)   The NEW dialog box will appear. Since Word Processor is already selected,

4. Press: (ENTER)   A blank word processing screen will appear.

This is the screen where you will create your memo to Chris.

This part of the document is to be prepared
with the Word Processing tool.

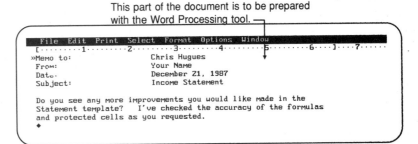

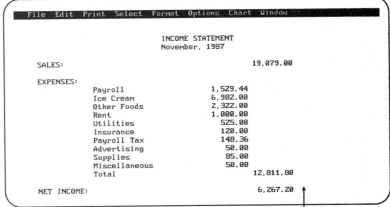

This part of the document will be taken from
the spreadsheet file you used before.

Figure 14-8

Changing the Margins

Because the default margins are greater than one inch, the completed document may not accommodate the width of the spreadsheet you are going to include; therefore, you must first decrease the size of the margins.

1. Press: (ALT) to enter the Menu bar.

2. Type: **p** (PRINT menu).

3. Type: **l** (LAYOUT option).

4. Press: (TAB) until the LEFT MARGIN field is highlighted.

5. Type: **1** to change the default of 1.3 to 1 inch.

6. Press: (TAB) to enter the RIGHT MARGIN field.

7. Type: **1** to change the default 1.2 to 1 inch.

8. Press: (TAB) until the FOOTER field is highlighted.

The Footer is set up to automatically number the pages of a document. To erase the automatic numbering of pages,

```
Memo to:  Chris Hughes
From:      Your Name
Date:      Today's Date
Subject:   Income Statement

Do you see any more improvements you would like made in the
Statement template?  I've checked the accuracy of the formulas
and protected cells as you requested.
```

Figure 14-9

9. **Press:** (DEL) to remove the Footer. Since the other settings are OK,

10. **Press:** (ENTER)

Typing the Memo

You are now ready to type the memo to Chris.

1. **Type the memo shown in Figure 14–9 and make the indicated substitutions for the italicized parts.**

2. Press: (ENTER) **twice** to place the cursor at the point where you want the spreadsheet to appear.

Opening the Spreadsheet Document

Before you can copy the spreadsheet, it must be resident in the computer's memory. That means you must open the file *STMENT.WKS*.

1. Press: (ALT) to enter the Menu bar. Since FILE is already highlighted,

2. Press: (ENTER)

3. Type: **o** (the letter "o" for the OPEN option).

4. Press: (TAB) **one time** to move the cursor to the FILES box.

5. Press: (↓) until *STMENT.WKS* is highlighted.

Note: STMENT.WKS may not appear in the FILES IN box if you have more than ten *Works* files on your data disk. As you press (↓), the list will scroll and *STMENT.WKS* will appear.

6. Press: (ENTER) The Income Statement will appear on the screen.

Copying the Spreadsheet

To cut out the entire spreadsheet for insertion into the memo,

1. Press: (CTRL)-(HOME) The cursor will be in Cell A1.

2. Press: (F8) to begin an extended selection.

3. Press: (CTRL)-(END) to highlight the entire spreadsheet.

4. Press: (ALT) to enter the Menu bar.

5. Type: **e** (EDIT menu).

6. Type: **c** (COPY option).

7. Look at the Prompt bar at the bottom of the screen.

The "Select new location and press ENTER..." message appears in the Prompt bar. To move the highlight to the new location in the memo and to copy the selected area,

8. Press: (ALT) until the Menu bar is highlighted.

9. Type: **w** (WINDOW menu).

10. Type the number next to the file called *WORD1.WPS*. Because you have not given the new word processing document a name, *Works* has assigned this temporary name for you. The cursor should still be two lines below your last typed line.

11. Press: (ENTER) to insert the spreadsheet which you copied. It may take a few seconds for the copy operation to be completed. Don't panic!

You can now add lines and make any other changes you may desire. *Important:* The copy of the spreadsheet that appears in your memo is now a part of the word processing document, just as if you had typed it in. Therefore, you cannot use it for calculations as you could when it was a spreadsheet.

Saving the File with a Different Name

As usual, you will want to save the file with a descriptive name like INCOME. Follow these instructions:

1. Press: (ALT) to enter the Menu bar.

2. Press: (ENTER) The FILE menu will drop down.

3. Type: **a** (SAVE AS... option). The SAVE AS dialog box will appear.

4. Look at the Current Drive field (line 2 in the dialog box). If it does not read A:\, follow steps a through c. Otherwise, continue to step 5.

   a. Press: (TAB) until the cursor moves to Other Drives & Directories.

   b. Press: (↓) until [-A-] is highlighted.

   c. Press: (ENTER) The Current Drive field will change to A:\

5. Type: **INCOME** The name will appear in the File Name field.

6. Press: (ENTER) The red light will glow on the floppy disk drive as the file is being saved.

Printing a File

To print a copy of your document, check to see that the printer is on and the paper is properly positioned.

1. Press: (ALT) to enter Menu bar.

2. Type: **p** to select PRINT menu. Since PRINT is already highlighted,

3. Press: (ENTER)

The PRINT dialog box appears.

4. Press: (ENTER) to accept the default setting of one copy.

More Scene Setting

Many times typographical errors are made and not detected during the course of writing. For this reason, many word processing programs incorporate a spelling checker. *Works* has such a spell check, and this section will demonstrate that capability.

1. Open the file named *SPELLCHK.WPS* (a word processing document). You will see the letter shown in Figure 14–10.

Note that some words have been deliberately misspelled. Use the Spell Checker to find and correct those errors.

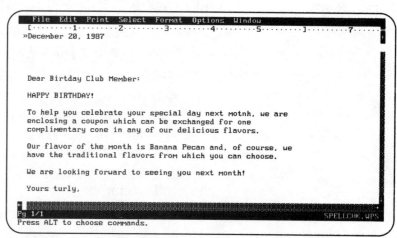

Figure14-10

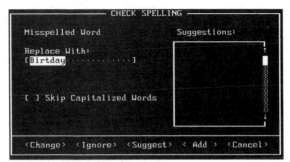

```
┌──────────────── CHECK SPELLING ──────────────────┐
│                                                    │
│  Misspelled Word              Suggestions:         │
│                                             ┌────┐↑│
│  Replace With:                              │    │ │
│  [Birtday············]                       │    │█│
│                                             │    │ │
│                                             │    │ │
│                                             │    │ │
│  [ ] Skip Capitalized Words                 │    │ │
│                                             │    │ │
│                                             │    │ │
│                                             │    │↓│
│                                             └────┘ │
│                                                    │
│  <Change>  <Ignore>  <Suggest>  < Add >  <Cancel> │
└────────────────────────────────────────────────────┘
```

Figure 14-11

Using the Spell Check Menu ▐▶

1. Press: (CTRL)-(HOME) to move the cursor to the beginning of the file if you are not already there.

2. Press: (ALT) to enter the Menu bar.

3. Type: **o** to select the OPTIONS menu.

4. Type: **c** to select the CHECK SPELLING option.

After a short time (in which the program will be searching for spelling errors by comparing each word in the file with the Spell Checker's dictionary), the CHECK SPELLING dialog box similar to Figure 14–11 will appear.

Note that the first unrecognized word ("Birtday" at the top of the screen) is highlighted, and the Replace With field shows that same unrecognized word. Pretend that this is a word for which you did not know the spelling.

5. Press: (TAB) until SUGGEST is highlighted.

6. Press: (ENTER)   The correct spelling will appear in the Suggestions box and the Replace With line.

7. Press: (ENTER) to make the replacement. If you do know the correct spelling, type that word when the dialog box appears. As soon as you start typing, the misspelled word disappears.

Works will continue to search the file for misspelled words. If that same word is misspelled again, the same replacement word is proposed in the Replace With text box. In that case, pressing (ENTER) is all that is necessary to make the change.

When all the misspelled words have been found, the following message will appear: "Check spelling finished."

8. Press: (ENTER) to accept completion of spell check.

Note: One of the options, "Skip Capitalized Words", was not necessary in this search. However, if you had a file containing many acronyms, you might wish to activate this option. To do so, use the ⊕ to place an X in the the box.

You will sometimes want to add words to the dictionary recognized by the spelling checker. For example, your name would not be recognized by the dictionary and the program would stop each time it occurs. Whenever the program stops at a word which you want added to the dictionary, press (TAB) to move the highlight to the *Add* option at the bottom, then press (ENTER). Whenever that name appears in the future, *Works* will accept it because that word has been added to the dictionary.

Review

If time permits, try some of the activities described in this chapter without looking at these directions.

Summary

Congratulations! You have practiced two of the basic integration operations, that is, merging addresses from a database file with a form letter in a word processing file, and transferring material from a spreadsheet file into a word processing document. Also, you have worked with four different files resident in the computer's memory at one time and used the spell check feature.

We are sure you can think of other applications for using the integration feature of *Works*. If you want to learn more, check with the *Works Reference* manual, or use the HELP or TUTORIAL features from the WINDOW menu.

Quitting *Works*

Follow these directions to quit *Works*:

1. Press: (ALT) to enter the Menu bar. Since FILE is already highlighted,

2. Press: (ENTER)

3. Type: **x** to exit. When *Works* asks if you want to save changes, choose the NO response.

4. Type: **cd** to change the Current Directory.

5. **Take your disk out of Drive A and place it in the protective envelope.**

6. **Turn the computer off.**

15 Communications

It is extremely important that this chapter be read carefully *before* sitting down before the computer.

Introduction

Computers can talk to each other! You can use a properly equipped computer to exchange messages with a friend or access the data and services of large computers anywhere in the world.

What's Possible?

With the Communications tool, you can
- Use electronic mail to send messages
- Search online databases for information
- Obtain current business, finance and investment information
- Conduct electronic conferences
- Shop electronically

What's Needed?

To send a message with a personal computer you need five things:
- computer
- modem
- communications software
- telephone line
- cables

Modem is short for modulation/demodulation. A modem is used to change the electronic signals of the sending computer to signals that can travel over telephone lines. This is called modulation.

Another modem is needed at the receiving end to convert the sound waves back to electronic signals which the computer can understand. This is called demodulation.

There are two types of modems: internal and external. Internal modems fit into slots inside the system unit. External modems are small boxes with phone cables or acoustic couplers which house standard telephone receivers.

To better understand how computers communicate, you may want to know how a modem transmits computer data. Personal computers use eight numbers or bits to represent one letter. For example the letter "A" is 01000001. The problem is that standard telephone lines can send the signal for only one bit at a time. To send the letter "A" over telephone lines, eight signals must be sent. The modem sends each signal sequentially (serially) through a device known as an **RS-232-C interface.** RS-232-C stands for "Recommended Standard number 232, version C."

One of the identifying features of a modem is the rate at which it transmits and receives data (its **baud rate**). The baud rates most commonly used are 300, 1200, 2400 and 9600. The baud rate of the modem at the sending computer must match that of the modem at the receiving computer.

Before you can begin communications, you must find out the baud rate of the receiving computer. You must set your communication software to conform to the baud rate, as well as several other important settings, sometimes called **parameters**. Information services usually publish their modem speed and you match that setting with your software. Other parameters have to do with checking for errors in transmission.

You don't have to understand what it all means—just type in the proper settings or parameters of the modem you are calling. The exercises in this chapter will lead you through the process of using one of the more popular information services.

Setting the Scene

The owner of your Ice Cream Factory, Chris Hughes, has decided that you and the managers of the other seven stores in the chain need to incorporate electronic communications in your operations.

The *Microsoft Works'* communications module contains basic features which enable you to call another computer or bulletin board, connect to a remote mainframe computer, or access information services.

These communications exercises will introduce you to the world of electronic communications through the use of CompuServe, one of the largest public information services. These exercises are not, however, meant to replace the CompuServe documentation. Chris chose CompuServe because it can be accessed through a local telephone number in major United States cities. You and your co-workers will be able to send and receive electronic mail, search for information, join electronic clubs and special interest groups, or even play games.

Getting Started

These exercises assume that your computer is properly equipped with a Hayes compatible modem and that the cabling and phone lines are connected. They also assume that you have established an account with CompuServe and that the necessary account information is available in the file *COMPUS.WCM*. We have included a *COMPUS.WCM* file on the data disk that comes with this book. That file is prepared with parameter settings that have been tested with an IBM PC computer, a Hayes 300/1200 baud modem, and a CompuServe account in the summer of 1988. In this worksheet you will be directed to investigate the parameters in that file and to change any that are site dependent.

If you wish to open your own individual account with CompuServe, please refer to the instructions in Appendix G, "Getting Started with CompuServe."

Checking the Parameters

The first thing you should do is check to see if the parameter settings in the *COMPUS.WCM* file are correct for your site and to make any changes that are necessary. To do that you must enter *Works* and open the *COMPUS.WCM* file.

Reminder: **Insert your data disk only when directed to do so**. Remember that the *Microsoft Works* program is stored on the hard disk in Drive C. The computer will look to Drive A initially in case you want to run a program other than one on Drive C. Your data disk contains only data; therefore, if your data disk is in Drive A before *Works* is loaded, an error message similar to "Non-system disk in Drive A" will be generated. The same message will appear if you attempt a warm boot with your data disk in Drive A.

1. Type: **cd\works**

2. Press: (ENTER)

3. Type: **works**

4. Press: (ENTER)   The NEW dialog box appears.

To begin this exercise you will use the *COMPUS.WCM* file that is stored on your data disk.

1. Press: (TAB) **two times** to move the cursor selection to <OPEN>.

2. Press: (ENTER)   An OPEN dialog box will appear.

3. **Put your data disk in disk Drive A.** (Don't forget to close the drive door).

4. Press: (TAB) to move the cursor to the middle box.

5. Press: ⬇ until [-A-] becomes highlighted.

6. Press: (ENTER) A list of file names will appear in the left-hand box.

7. Press: (TAB) until the cursor moves to the right-hand box.

8. Press: ⬇ to move the cursor to the Communications line.

9. Press: (ENTER) The OPEN dialog box appears. As you can see, only one communications file is listed.

10. Press: (TAB) to move the cursor to the left-hand box.

11. Press: ⬇ to select the *COMPUS.WCM* file.

12. Press: (ENTER) The COMMUNICATIONS menu bar will appear on the screen. Look at Figure 15–1 to see the different screen components.

Look at the screen. On the right bottom of the screen is displayed the name of the current communication file, *COMPUS.WCM*. The bottom line of the screen is called the ***Status bar***. The Status bar also contains the word, ***OFFLINE***, in the lower left corner. Offline means that you are not connected to another computer. While you are off line you will investigate the *COMPUS.WCM* file and change any parameter settings that are needed for your particular installation.

Changing the Phone Number

1. Press: (ALT) to enter the Menu bar

2. Type: **O** to select the OPTION menu. The OPTION menu allows you to change the communications settings.

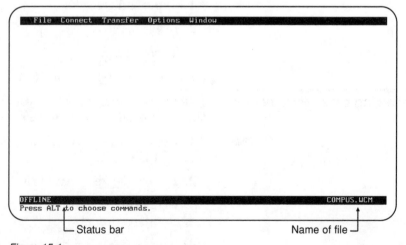

Figure 15-1

```
┌─────────────────────── PHONE ───────────────────────┐
│                                                      │
│  Phone Number: [9,9,988 8762··················]       │
│                                                      │
│  Modem Setup:  [······························]       │
│                                                      │
│  Dial Type:                                          │
│  ┌──────────────────────────┐                        │
│  │ (·) Tone  ( ) Pulse      │  [ ] Automatic Answer  │
│  └──────────────────────────┘                        │
│                                                      │
│                          <   OK   >   <Cancel>       │
└──────────────────────────────────────────────────────┘
```

Figure 15-2

3. Type: **P**   The PHONE dialog box will appear. (See Figure 15–2.)

4. **Look at the telephone number listed on the screen.** It is the CompuServe number valid for the 408 area code. The 408 area code encompasses San Jose, California, and surrounding areas.

5. **Notice the two 9's separated by commas from the rest of the number**. The 9's were needed to get an outside line from the authors' test site and the commas cause the communications software to generate pauses while dialing the number.

6. **Type the phone number** you will use in your area to access CompuServe.

7. Press: (TAB) until the cursor is in the Dial Type box. Leave Tone selected if you have a touch tone phone. If you have a dial phone, use the (→) to move the selection to Pulse.

8. Press: (TAB) until <OK> is selected.

9. Press: (ENTER) to complete entering the number.

Viewing other Parameters

If a blank communications screen is not displayed, press (ENTER). To view other parameters,

1. Press: (ALT)

2. Press: **o**   The OPTIONS menu will drop down.

3. Press: **c**   The COMMUNICATIONS dialog box similar to Figure 15–3 will appear.

The COMMUNICATIONS dialog box allows you to enter the settings of the computer with which you wish to communicate.

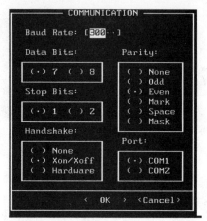

Figure 15-3

Remember that the two computers must have compatible settings. The dialog box should show the following parameter settings.

Baud Rate: 300
Data Bits: 7
Stop Bits: 1
Handshake: Xon/Xoff
Parity: Even
Port: COM1

4. If the COMMUNICATIONS dialog box does not show the parameter settings listed above, follow steps 5 through 14 to enter the correct parameters. If the parameters are already correct, skip to step 15.

5. Type: **300**   This is the least expensive rate.

6. Press: (TAB) to move the cursor to the Data Bits box.

7. Press: (←) to select 7 bits

8. Press: (TAB) to move the cursor to the Stop Bit box. The setting should be 1.

9. Press: (←) to select 1.

10. Press: (TAB) to move the cursor to the Parity Box.

11. Press: (↑) or (↓) until Even is selected.

12. Press: (TAB) to move the cursor to the Handshake box. Xon/Xoff should be selected.

13. Press: (TAB) to move to the Port box. COM1 should be selected to send serial data through Communications line 1.

14. Press: (TAB) to <OK>.

15. Press: (ENTER) to complete setting the parameters.

Saving the Parameters

If you have made any changes in the parameter settings you need to save them. By saving the settings you do not have to reenter the information each time you want to log on to Compu-Serve.

1. Press: (ALT)

2. Type: **f** to select FILE.

3. Type: **s** to select SAVE.

In order to call CompuServe, all you have to do is open the file *COMPUS.WCM* and connect. You do not have to enter this phone number or the settings again; the computer will recall the phone number for you.

You are now ready to log on—but before you do, make note of the following procedures in case the computer does not behave as you would expect.

Handling Unexpected Problems

If you want to quit at any time during the logging on process, enter the Menu bar and select CONNECT. Then type **B** to select Break.

If the connection was not successful, you will get the message: "NO CARRIER". It is probable that the phone line was busy. Select the CONNECT menu again and type **D** to dial again. If you are not successful after a few tries, check the phone number and settings under the OPTIONS menu to see if you typed them correctly.

Connecting to CompuServe

Before actually calling CompuServe, write your user ID and passwords in the spaces provided below so you will not have to waste time "on line" looking them up in the next section. CompuServe charges users for connect time, so you should make sure you plan your sessions to stay connected as few minutes as possible.

User ID No.:_____

Password: _____

You are finally ready to make your first call.

1. Press: (ALT) to enter the Menu bar.

2. Type: **c** to choose CONNECT. Since the CONNECT option you need is already highlighted,

3. Press: (ENTER)

A clock at the bottom of the screen records the seconds while you are waiting to connect. If the connection is successful, the word "CONNECT" will appear on the screen.

4. Press: (CTRL)-C

Entering the User ID Number and Password

As soon as a successful connection is made you will be asked for your user ID number and password.

1. **Type your user ID number.**

2. Press: (ENTER) You are now asked for the password.

3. **Type your password.** For security reasons, the letters you type will not appear on the screen.

4. Press: (ENTER)

5. If the message "invalid entry" appears, type the password again.

Viewing the Menus

The CompuServe NEW menu will appear. Notice that an exclamation point (!, CompuServe's prompt character) appears at the end of the on-screen text. Follow the steps below to obtain the TOP menu (CompuServe's main menu):

1. Type: **Go Top**

2. Press: (ENTER) A TOP menu similar to Figure 15–4 will appear. This menu can be accessed at any time by typing Go Top at the exclamation point. Always wait for the exclamation point prompt before typing any command.

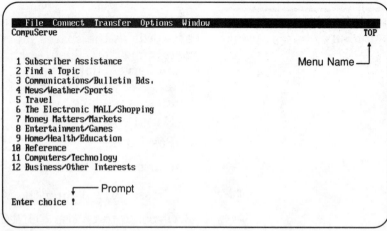

Figure 15-4

The word at the top right corner of the screen of each menu is the name of that menu. By typing Go followed by the menu name at the exclamation point (for example, Go Top or Go News) you go directly to that menu. By selecting one of the twelve topics from the TOP menu you will be taken to another menu.

Understanding the Menu Tree

Each menu gives you other menu choices. This is called a tree format with each menu branching to another menu. You can go back to any menu by typing Go and the word which was at the top right corner of the menu. Remember, the first menu was called TOP.

Take the time now to try any of the menu options and tour the services which interest you. Simply type the identifying number and press (ENTER). Jot down the word in the right corner of a menu if you want to return to it later using the GO command.

Remember: If you get into trouble, press (CTRL)-C to interrupt the action and then type **Go Top** to return to the top main menu.

When you are finished touring, return to this worksheet.

More Scene Setting

One of the reasons Chris gave all managers an account on CompuServe was so they could communicate with each other easily and at any time of the day. In this exercise you will learn how to leave electronic mail messages for others and how to retrieve your own messages.

Mail Message

You are to send a message to yourself and read it the next time you log on. First you have to go to the TOP main menu and select the Communications/Bulletin Board option. Follow the instructions carefully.

1. Type: **Go Top** to return to the main menu

2. Press: (ENTER)

3. Type: **3** to select Communications/Bulletin Bds. If you ever want to reach this menu directly, type Go Communicate at the ! prompt.

4. Press: (ENTER)

5. Type: **1** to select EasyPlex Electronic Mail. If you want to reach this menu at any future time, type Go EasyPlex at the ! prompt.

6. Press: (ENTER)

7. Type: **2** to obtain a screen on which you can compose a new message.

8. Press: (ENTER) to obtain the message screen.

The lines of the message screen are numbered. Follow the directions below to create a message. If you prefer, create your own. This program does not wordwrap so you must press (ENTER) after each line of your message. To finish the message, type **/exit** on a separate line.

⏵ **1.** Type: **This is my first electronic message**.

2. Press: (ENTER)

3. Type: **It is an adventure.**

4. Press: (ENTER)

5. Type: **/exit**

6. Press: (ENTER)

To send the message,

⏵ **1.** Type: **1**

2. Press: (ENTER)　　Follow CompuServe's prompts and

3. **Type your user ID number.**

4. Press: (ENTER)

5. Type: **Hello** or another appropriate subject line.

6. Press: (ENTER)

7. **Type your first name at the prompt "Your name:___"**

8. Press: (ENTER)

9. Type: **Y** to verify the message.

10. Press: (ENTER)　　(The initials <CR> in the prompt line is CompuServe's symbol for the (ENTER) key; however, since we will be quitting CompuServe at this point, continue with the following instructions).

The next time you log on to CompuServe a message will be waiting for you.

Quitting CompuServe

To quit at any time, type Bye at the ! prompt. If you ever get disconnected accidentally, immediately call the service and log off.

1. Type: **bye**
2. Press: (ENTER)

Disconnecting *Works*

To disconnect, you must repeat the same steps you used to connect. It is always a good idea to log off of a service before disconnecting. Most information services charge by the minute and you may be charged for the time it takes for the service to determine that you have hung up.

1. Press: (ALT)
2. Type: **C** to select the CONNECT menu. Since Connect is a toggle,
3. Press: (ENTER) to disconnect.
4. Press: (ENTER) to confirm disconnection.

Temporarily Quitting *Works*

You will exit *Works* now so that you can review the log-on procedure and retrieve your message in the next exercise.

1. Press: (ALT) to enter the Menu bar. Since FILE is already highlighted,
2. Press: (ENTER)
3. Type: **x** to select the EXIT option. If the message "OK to disconnect?" appears, press (ENTER) again.
4. **Take your disk out of Drive A and place it in the protective envelope.**
5. **Leave the computer on.**

More Scene Setting

As you work through this exercise, you will continue your exploration of the CompuServe system. You will learn how to browse through bulletin board messages, and how to retrieve your own messages.

Reopening the *Compus* File

First, load *Works* from Drive C. With the C> displayed,

1. Type: **works**
2. Press: (ENTER)

To begin this exercise you will again use the *COMPUS.WCM* file that is stored on your data disk.

3. Press: (TAB) **two times** to move the cursor selection to <OPEN>.

4. Press: (ENTER) An OPEN dialog box will appear.

5. **Put your data disk in Disk Drive A.**

6. Press: (TAB) until the cursor moves to the middle box.

7. Press: (↓) until [-A-] becomes highlighted.

8. Press: (ENTER) A list of file names from Drive A will appear in the left-hand box.

9. Press: (TAB) until the cursor moves to the right-hand box.

10. Press: (↓) to move the cursor to the Communications line.

11. Press: (ENTER) The OPEN dialog box with only Communications files listed will appear.

12. Press: (TAB) to move the cursor to the left-hand box.

13. Press: (↓) until the file name *COMPUS.WCM* is highlighted.

14. Press: (ENTER) The *COMPUS.WCM* file will be loaded and the COMMUNICATION menu bar will appear on the screen.

In this exercise you will also be using the Capture feature of the *Works* Communications module. Capture allows you to record everything that is displayed on the screen during a session on CompuServe and save it as a word processing file. Later you can view and edit the information and save what you think is important.

Turning on Capture   IIII➡

1. Press: (ALT)

2. Type: **T** to select the TRANSFER menu.

3. Type: **C** to select the CAPTURE TEXT option.

4. Type: **A:capture.wps** This name causes the information that is displayed on the screen to be saved on the disk located in Drive A under the file name *CAPTURE.WPS*. You should always save captured text files with ".WPS" extensions so that *Works* can recognize them as word processing files.

5. Press: (ENTER)

6. **Look at the center of the Status bar at the bottom of the screen.** The word "Capture" tells you that the incoming information will be saved on your disk.

Connecting to CompuServe

After you sign on, you will browse through some messages left by other CompuServe users and will retrieve the message you left for yourself in the last exercise.

 1. Press: (ALT)

2. Type: **C** to select CONNECT.

3. Press: (ENTER)   If connection is made, the word "CONNECT" will appear on the screen.

4. Press: (CTRL)-C   You will be asked for your user ID number.

5. **Type your user ID number.**

6. Press: (ENTER)   You will be asked for the password.

7. **Type your password.** The letters you type will not appear on the screen.

8. Press: (ENTER)   If the message "invalid entry" appears, type the password again.

Every time you are signed on you will be informed of any electronic messages that are waiting for you. The EASYPLEX MESSAGE menu informs you that a message is awaiting your attention. You can read the messages as soon as you begin a session, or you can go on to another activity and read your messages later.

For this exercise you will delay reading your own mail until you have read some messages that are on the electronic bulletin board.

Viewing the Bulletin Board

Any time you start a new activity in CompuServe, you should start with the TOP menu. The following instructions begin there and lead you down through the menus to the Bulletin Board. If you are not in the TOP Menu,

 1. Type: **Go Top**

2. Press: (ENTER)   You are now at the TOP menu. To browse through a few of its menus,

3. Type: **3** for Communications.

4. Press: (ENTER)   The COMMUNICATE menu will appear.

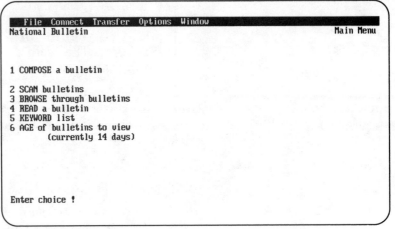

```
┌──────────────────────────────────────────────────────────────┐
│  File  Connect  Transfer  Options  Window                      │
│ National Bulletin                                    Main Menu  │
│                                                                │
│                                                                │
│ 1 COMPOSE a bulletin                                           │
│                                                                │
│ 2 SCAN bulletins                                               │
│ 3 BROWSE through bulletins                                     │
│ 4 READ a bulletin                                              │
│ 5 KEYWORD list                                                 │
│ 6 AGE of bulletins to view                                     │
│         (currently 14 days)                                    │
│                                                                │
│                                                                │
│                                                                │
│ Enter choice !                                                 │
│                                                                │
└──────────────────────────────────────────────────────────────┘
```

Figure 15-5

5. Type: **4** for National Bulletin Board.

6. Press: (ENTER)   Some information about the bulletin board will appear.

7. Press: (ENTER) as directed by the screen prompt <CR> and the BULLETIN BOARD main menu appears on the screen. (See Figure 15–5.)

8. Type: **3** to choose BROWSE from NAT BULL Menu.

9. Press: (ENTER) and a menu similar to Figure 15–6 will appear.

The notices are listed under three categories. In our example there are 352 sale items, 310 wanted items and 321 notices.

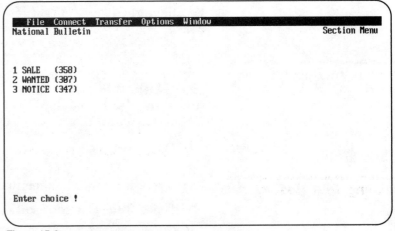

```
┌──────────────────────────────────────────────────────────────┐
│  File  Connect  Transfer  Options  Window                      │
│ National Bulletin                                 Section Menu  │
│                                                                │
│                                                                │
│ 1 SALE   (358)                                                 │
│ 2 WANTED (307)                                                 │
│ 3 NOTICE (347)                                                 │
│                                                                │
│                                                                │
│                                                                │
│                                                                │
│                                                                │
│                                                                │
│ Enter choice !                                                 │
│                                                                │
└──────────────────────────────────────────────────────────────┘
```

Figure 15-6

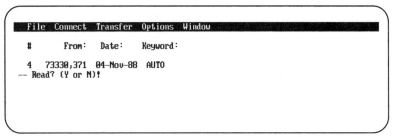

Figure 15-7

Your numbers will be different. To read about some of the sale items,

10. Type: **1**

11. Press: (ENTER)   A message appears asking you to "Enter keyword (for example, book) or <CR> for all:" When a message is added to the bulletin board it is given a keyword by the person who initiated the message. Even though you don't know what the keywords are, you can still browse through a few messages as follows:

12. Press: (ENTER)   A screen similar to Figure 15-7 will appear.

You now have to make a decision about what you want to do. From this screen you can either read the message currently described, get another message description, or return to the NATIONAL BULLETIN BOARD menu.

13. Decide which action you wish to take and respond accordingly. Your three choices are listed below:

   a. Type: **N** to cause the next message description to be displayed.

   b. Type: **Y** to cause the current message and the sender's ID to be displayed. If, after reading the message, you decide to follow up on it, you should remember the sender's identification number so you can communicate with him/her when you are finished with the bulletin board items.

   c. Type: **X** (must be a capital letter) to return to the NATIONAL BULLETIN BOARD menu.

14. Press: (ENTER) after selecting one of the above choices.

Reading Your Messages

You must be in the EASYPLEX menu in order to read messages addressed to you. At the ! prompt,

▮▮▶   **1.** Type: **Go Easyplex**

2. Press: (ENTER)

3. Type: **1** to read the first message.

4. Press: (ENTER)

Deleting a Message

Many times you will want to delete a message after reading it. Unnecessary messages merely clutter up your mail box. You can delete messages by using the EASYPLEX ACTION menu.

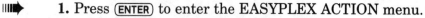

1. Press (ENTER) to enter the EASYPLEX ACTION menu.

2. Type: **1** to select the DELETE option.

3. Press: (ENTER) to delete message #1.

The EASYPLEX menu appears again to allow you to leave another message. The "!" prompt should appear. Whenever you see that prompt, you can go to another menu. In the next section you will switch to another menu.

Checking Cost

You may want to know how much has been spent on CompuServe so far. Remember that the charge is calculated per minute. You must be in the MONTH menu to check current charges. Since the MONTH menu does not appear as one of your current menu choices,

1. Type: **Go month**

2. Press: (ENTER)

3. Type: **2**

4. Press: (ENTER) A summary of your account's charges should appear.

Quitting CompuServe

You will now end this exercise by logging off CompuServe and looking at the file you just captured. To log off,

1. Type: **bye**

2. Press: (ENTER)

Turning Off the Capture Feature

Now that you are off line you need to take *Works* out of the CAPTURE mode.

1. Press: (ALT)

2. Type: **T** to select TRANSFER.

3. Type: **E** to end Capture Text. The word "Capture" disappears from the center bottom of the screen.

Reading the Captured File

You can work with the captured file just as you would with any other word processing file. The following steps will remind you how to open the file so you can read it.

1. Press: (ALT)

2. Type: **f** to open the FILE menu.

3. Type: **o** to select OPEN.

4. Type: **A:capture.wps**

5. Press: (ENTER)   When the OPEN AS dialog box appears, accept the WORD PROCESSOR option.

6. Press: (ENTER)   The first screenful of the captured file will appear on the screen.

7. Press: (PGDN) to see additional sections of the file.

Quitting *Works*

When you finish using a program, it is always best to formally quit the program. If you do not follow that procedure, information may be lost because the computer updates the directories on the disks during the quitting process. The following instructions will guide you through the steps for quitting *Works*.

1. Press: (ALT) to enter the Menu bar. Since FILE is already highlighted,

2. Press: (ENTER)

3. Type: **x** to select the EXIT option. If the message "OK to disconnect?" appears, press (ENTER) again.

4. **Take your disk out of Drive A and place it in the protective envelope.**

5. **Turn the computer off.**

Introducing the IBM PC

Introducing the IBM PC

If you are unfamiliar with the IBM PC, you should become acquainted with a few basic functions before working with *Microsoft Works*. This worksheet will help you learn about the computer as you complete some selected exercises from the "Exploring the IBM" disk that accompanies the machine.

Getting Started

To begin this session, obtain a copy of **"Exploring the IBM"** and station yourself before an IBM personal computer.

1. **Insert the "Exploring the IBM" disk into Drive A and close the drive door.** Starting the computer depends on the state of the computer. **Check your computer and continue with step 2 or 3**, whichever is appropriate.

2. **If the computer is OFF find the On/Off switch located on the right side of the system unit (near the back) and switch it ON.** This is called a *cold boot.* **Continue with step 4.**

3. **If the computer is ON** hold down the (CTRL) and (ALT) keys with your left hand, and keep holding them down while you press the (DEL) key. **Release** all three keys. This is called a *warm boot* and will restart the computer.

4. **WAIT while the computer does a self check of the system.** This will take a few seconds and the red lights on both drives will light up from time to time, indicating that software is being transferred into memory from the disks. Eventually, an IBM Greeting complete with sound effects will appear on the screen, followed by a few introductory screens and finally you will see a menu similar to one of those shown in Figure A-1.

5. The "Exploring the IBM" disk is divided into chapters.

    a. If you are using an XT computer, do the following chapters: "Instructions," "The Keyboard," "The Printer," and "Funwriter" (Chapters 1, 2, 3 and 4). *Note:* DO NOT use

```
CHAPTER SELECTION MENU          TABLE OF CONTENTS

1.   Instructions              1.   Instructions
2.   The Keyboard              2.   Keyboard
3.   The Printer               3.   Disk Storage & DOS
4.   Funwriter                 4.   BASIC Programming
5.   Disk Storage & DOS        5.   Printer
6.   BASIC Programming
7.   The End
```

Figure A-1

the printer for Chapter 3, just read the descriptions of printer operations on the screen.

b. If you are using a PC computer, just do Chapters 1 and 2, "Instructions," and "The Keyboard."

6. Return to this worksheet when you see the Title Screen for the chapter entitled "Disk Storage & DOS".

Quitting "Exploring the IBM"

Welcome back! Because "Exploring the IBM" is a structured tutorial program, it is not necessary for you to formally quit the program. Just remove the disk from the drive and turn off the computer.

Hardware Components of the IBM Personal Computer

Five major hardware components make up an IBM personal computer system: **Screen, Keyboard, System Unit, Disk Drives,** and **Printer.** Figure A–2 below shows all components except the Printer.

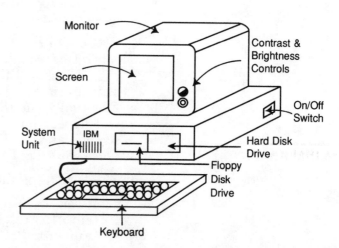

Figure A-2

The screen may also be called a *monitor* or a *CRT* (Cathode Ray Tube). There are three major types of monitors: monochrome (one color), RGB (red, green, blue) and EGA (enhanced graphics adapter). Monochrome (one color) displays are more popular for word processing because the letters are clearer on them than on most color displays.

There are two basic types of IBM keyboards. The PC keyboard has the function keys on the left side. The AT/XT keyboard has the function keys on the top and has separate number and arrow keys.

If you opened the computer's system unit you would find the *mother board* at the bottom of the unit. The mother board is the main circuit board into which many chips and circuit boards are plugged. The most important chip on the mother board is the *CPU chip* because it controls the sequence of activities in the computer. The CPU (Central Processing Unit) chip or microprocessor is the "brain" of the computer. *Memory* chips are of two types: *ROM and RAM.* ROM (read only memory) stores information permanently. RAM (random access memory) storage is temporary; the information disappears when the computer is turned off. The amount of RAM memory determines the storage capacity of the computer. RAM memory is usually measured in units of *kilobytes* or *megabytes*. A kilobyte (usually referred to as 1K) can store approximately 1000 characters; while a megabyte (referred to in computer jargon as 1 meg) can store 1 million characters.

The *disk drives* are usually housed in the system unit. This book assumes that you have one floppy disk drive (A) and one hard or fixed disk drive (C). Information is saved magnetically on the disks to be recalled for later use.

The two main classifications of *printers* are impact and non impact. Impact printers have a mechanism which hits the paper. Some examples are dot matrix and daisy wheel printers. Examples of non impact printers are ink jet, thermal and laser.

Without looking at the illustration on the previous page, try to label the components of the Microcomputer system shown in Figure A–3. Check your answers with Figure A–2 when you finish.

The IBM Keyboard

The main portion of the IBM keyboard is laid out similar to a typewriter. However, there are several important auxiliary keys with which you must be familiar. Also, the marking on some of the more common keys is not the same as you will find on other computer keyboards. The keys listed below are important. *Note*: Some of these keys are marked *toggle switch*. When you use a

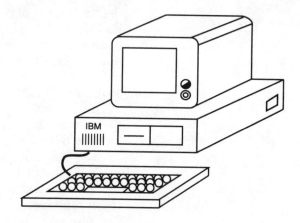

Figure A-3

toggle switch key the first time, it turns the activity on; when you press it again, it turns off the activity.

 FUNCTION KEYS (F1 through F10) are found on the left side of the keyboard on the IBM PC and along the top row of the keyboard on the IBM AT. The purpose of the function keys change with each program. **Do not use the function keys unless you are explicitly directed to do so.**

 ESCAPES from the current to the previous activity. Sometimes when you are in trouble the ESC key will rescue you.

 SHIFT key for upper case letters. Hold down the SHIFT key while typing another key, then release both keys.

 Locks the letter keys to produce capital letters. **CAPS LOCK** is a toggle switch key.

 TAB key.

 BACKSPACE key.

ENTER or **RETURN** key.

NUMBER LOCK key controls the number keypad on the right side of the keyboard. NUM LOCK is a toggle switch key that switches between (1) activating the number keys and (2) activating the arrow keys and the other alternate features of the number keypad. (The AT/XT keyboard has separate arrow keys not controlled by the NUM LOCK key.)

CURSOR MOVEMENT keys control the movement of the screen cursor.

INSERT key is used for inserting text in some applications.

CONTROL key is used in conjunction with other keys to perform various activities. When the NUM LOCK key is off, CTRL is used in conjunction with ALT and DEL to restart the computer. Do not use the CONTROL key unless explicitly directed to do so.

DELETE key is used for deleting text in some applications. Also used in conjunction with ALT and CTRL to control the actions of the computer. Do not use the DELETE key unless explicitly directed to do so.

ALTERNATE key is used to change the effect of some of the other keys. Also used in conjunction with DEL and CTRL to control the actions of the computer. Do not use the ALTERNATE key unless explicitly directed to do so.

WARM BOOT restarts the system. Hold down CTRL and ALT while pressing DEL, then release all three keys.

PrtSc
*

PRINTS what is on the screen to the printer. The PC keyboard requires that the SHIFT key be held down simultaneously with the PRTSC key.

Scroll Lock

Stops the screen from scrolling. To continue, press the space bar.

The Disk Drives

Personal computers use two types of disks to store information: flexible disks (floppy) and permanent disks (hard). Floppy disks hold about 400,000 characters of information or about 120 single-spaced pages of text. Your data disk is a floppy disk. Floppy disks can be inserted or removed from the floppy disk drive any time that the RED DISK DRIVE light is **NOT** on. Many systems have two floppy drives.

Hard disks are not removable from the system unit. The disks are rigid metal coated with metallic oxide. Fixed disks have the advantage of greater storage capacity and increased speed in saving and retrieving data.

A disk drive can either read data from or write data to a magnetic disk. Each disk drive has a name such as A, B, or C. The drive name is used to instruct the system where to read or write data. If you have two floppy disk drives, they are generally named Drive A and Drive B. If you have a built-in hard disk drive, it is usually called Drive C.

Figure A-4

Label
Protective Jacket

Write Protect Notch

Spindle Hole

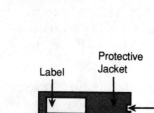

Read/Write Access Slot

B Laboratory Procedures

The following rules are designed to protect your computer and to help prevent the loss of *your* valuable time and data. By protecting the equipment, more computers will be available for you to use more of the time.

Do's

- The computer is on a very restricted diet. Do keep food, gum or drinks out of the lab.
- Leave the computer on unless directed otherwise.
- Turn the computer off before moving the computer or electrical connections. You could accidentally unplug the computer and lose work in progress.
- Do treat the computers with the care you would give any expensive electronic device.
- Do feel free to ask questions of your classroom neighbors, the lab assistant, if there is one, and your instructor.

Disk Handling

Some authors use the word, *diskette,* instead of the more common term, *disk.* We prefer "disk" and use that term throughout this document. In some cases you may see the alternate form, "diskette", shown on your computer screen—it depends on the program currently being used. In any event, the two words mean exactly the same thing—a device used for the electronic storage of information used by the computer. Disks for the IBM PC look like Figure B–1.

Label — Protective Jacket

Write Protect Notch

Spindle Hole

Read/Write Access Slot

Figure B-1

When the *write protect notch* is covered, the IBM cannot write or erase any information on the disk. However, it can still read information from the disk.

The disks used by the IBM are quite fragile and certain precautions must be taken to protect the disks and the programs and data contained on the disks.

- Keep floppy disks away from: magnets, magnetized objects, telephones, or electric motors; excessive heat or sunlight; dust, dirt, and moisture.
- Avoid placing heavy objects on the disk.
- When the disk is not in the disk drive, be sure it is in its envelope.
- Use a soft tip pen when writing on the disk label. DO NOT use a ball point pen or a pencil.

C Using MS/DOS

Setting the Scene

Normally, when you turn on an IBM PC the first thing you must do is load a group of programs that help you manage the computer's resources. This group of programs is called DOS for *Disk Operating System*. In this Appendix we are assuming that you have DOS already installed on your hard disk. DOS programs help you handle the screen, printer, keyboard, and the transfer of data and application programs into and out of memory. Among other things, DOS makes it possible for you to

- Load files
- Copy disks
- List the names of the files on a disk
- Format blank disks

When you turn on your computer, certain of the DOS programs are transferred from the hard disk into the computer's main memory. These DOS programs allow you to use other programs. Once loaded, DOS sits in the computer waiting for your instructions.

In this worksheet you will learn how to:

- Access DOS
- Enter the date and time
- List a directory of files
- Use some selected DOS commands
- Change the active disk drive
- Copy files
- Check the status of a disk
- Check the version of DOS

Introducing Disk Storage and DOS

In this section of this worksheet you will be using the "Exploring the IBM" software that you used in Appendix A. Follow the instructions given below to get started.

 1. **Insert the "EXPLORING THE IBM" disk into Drive A and close the drive door.** Starting the computer depends

on the state of the computer. **Check your computer and continue with step 2 or 3**, whichever is appropriate.

2. **If the computer is OFF, find the On/Off switch located on the right side of the system unit (near the back) and switch it ON.** This is called a *cold boot*. **Continue with step 4.**

3. **If the computer is ON,** hold down the (CTRL) and (ALT) keys with your left hand, and keep holding them down while you press the (DEL) key. **Release** all three keys. This is called a *warm boot* and will restart the computer.

4. **WAIT while the computer does a self check of the system.** This will take a few seconds and the red lights on both drives will light up from time to time, indicating that software is being transferred into memory from the disks. Eventually, an IBM greeting, complete with sound effects, will appear on the screen, followed by a few introductory screens and finally you will see a menu similar to one of those shown in Figure C–1. This menu is for illustration only.

5. Press: (ALT) and (PGDN) together to return to the chapter selection menu (Figure C-1).

6. Press: (↓) to select the chapter entitled "Disk Storage and DOS."

7. Press: (ENTER) to start the lessons in the chapter. The "Disk Storage and DOS" chapter will be the only lesson you will do during this session.

8. **Complete all the pages in the chapter by pressing** (PGDN) whenever you are ready to go on to the next page.

9. **Follow all the instructions as they appear.**

CHAPTER SELECTION MENU

1. Instructions
2. The Keyboard
3. The Printer
4. Funwriter
5. Disk Storage & DOS
6. BASIC Programming
7. The End

TABLE OF CONTENTS

1. Instructions
2. Keyboard
3. Disk Storage & DOS
4. BASIC Programming
5. Printer

Figure C-1

10. **When you finish** the "Disk Storage & DOS" chapter, and "BASIC Programming" appears, press (ALT) and (PGDN) together to return to the Chapter Selection menu.

11. Press: (↓) until "The End" is highlighted.

12. Press: (ENTER) to see a screen titled "What's Next".

13. **Take out the disk in Drive A.**

14. Press: (CTRL)-(ALT) and (DEL) keys together to return to the IBM prompt.

Using DOS on Your Own

In this section you will have an opportunity to use some of the DOS commands. Some of the more common ones are:

DIR   Lists the files on a disk
FORMAT   Formats a disk and erases old files
COPY   Copies one or more files
DISKCOPY   Formats and copies an entire disk

Formatting

To *format* a disk means to write a special pattern on the disk so that it can be used for information storage. If you are using 5-1/4" floppy disks, that special pattern consists of 40 concentric circles called *tracks* and 9 wedge shaped sections called *sectors*. New blank disks cannot be used to store information; they must be formatted before they are used. Information is electronically stored along the tracks and can be accessed according to a track and sector address scheme. (See Figure C-2.)

The Directory

One type of information that is always stored on one of the tracks is called the ***directory.*** A directory is simply a list of the files that are stored on the disk, together with their disk address and other important information about each file. If the format command is applied to a disk that already contains some information, it **erases** all of the files on the disk and sets up a new directory.

Diskcopy Command

The diskcopy command formats the receiving disk first; then copies all of the files on one disk to the newly formatted one, thus making an exact duplicate. Do not format your data disk or use it as the recipient of a diskcopy because all of your files will be erased!

Getting Started with DOS ⏵

1. **Turn on the computer.** When you turn on your computer, the DOS programs will be transferred into memory from the hard disk and the DOS prompt appears on the screen.

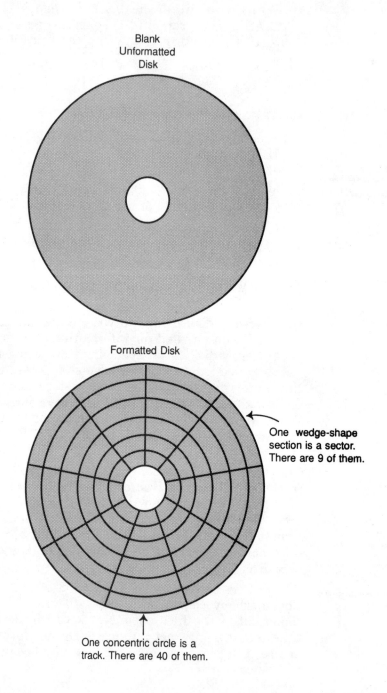

Blank
Unformatted
Disk

Formatted Disk

One wedge-shape
section is a sector.
There are 9 of them.

One concentric circle is a
track. There are 40 of them.

Figure C-2

The first thing DOS wants to know is the date and time. A screen similar to the following one will appear.

```
Current date is Tues 9-23-1987
Enter new date (mm-dd-yy):
```

Figure C-3

Entering the Date

In the instructions that follow, we are assuming that the date you wish to enter is March 7, 1988. Please do not modify the instructions. We want you to type in the wrong date.

⟶ 1. Type: **3** (for the month). Use the numbers at the top of the keyboard.

2. Type: **-** (a hyphen).

3. Type: **7** (for the day).

4. Type: **-** (a hyphen).

5. Type: **88** (for the year).

6. Press: (ENTER)

The screen should be similar to Figure C–4.

```
Current date is Wed 1-02-1980
Enter new date (mm-dd-yy): 3-7-88
C>
```

Figure C-4

Entering the Time

In the instructions that follow, we are assuming that the time is 3:30 P.M. Later in this worksheet you will have an opportunity to enter the correct time and date.

⟶ 1. Type: **15** (for 3 P.M. in 24-hour time).

2. Type: **:** (a colon).

3. Type: **30** (for minutes).

4. Press: (ENTER)

You could, if you wish, enter the time correct to seconds and hundredths of seconds, but that level of accuracy is not necessary for most normal applications. The computer will now keep time for you and "stamp" your files with the current date and time whenever you save information on a disk.

The "C>" on the screen is called the ***prompt.*** It means that DOS is currently working with Drive C. The blinking cursor means that DOS is waiting for your next command.

Changing the Time and Date

The date and times you entered are not correct. You will correct them in this section. The C> should be displayed.

1. Type: **date**

2. Press: (ENTER)

3. Type the current date in month, day, year format.

4. Press: (ENTER)

5. Type: **time**

6. Press: (ENTER)

7. Type the current time using the 24-hour clock.

8. Press: (ENTER)

9. Type: **date**

10. Press: (ENTER)

11. If the date is correct, press (ENTER) Otherwise, correct the date.

12. Type: **time**

13. Press: (ENTER)

14. **If the time is correct, press** (ENTER) Otherwise, correct the time.

Looking at the Directory

Now, let's find out the names of the DOS files on Drive C. The C> prompt should be showing.

1. Type: **dir** (it doesn't matter if it is typed in capitals or not).

2. Press: (ENTER)

The list will scroll by very quickly. The end of the list will appear, similar to Figure C–5.

The first two columns list the files' names and extensions. The third column describes the size of the file. The fourth and fifth columns list the date and times the files were created or modified. At the bottom of the screen are listed the number of files and the amount of storage space left on the disk.

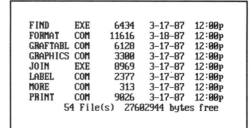

```
FIND      EXE     6434    3-17-87  12:00p
FORMAT    COM    11616    3-18-87  12:00p
GRAFTABL  COM     6128    3-17-87  12:00p
GRAPHICS  COM     3300    3-17-87  12:00p
JOIN      EXE     8969    3-17-87  12:00p
LABEL     COM     2377    3-17-87  12:00p
MORE      COM      313    3-17-87  12:00p
PRINT     COM     9026    3-17-87  12:00p
     54 File(s)   27602944 bytes free
```

Figure C-5

Viewing a Directory with the Pause Option

To display one screen of the directory at a time, use the directory command with a pause. With the C> displayed

1. Type: **dir/p**

2. Press: (ENTER) One screen full of directory information will appear and at the bottom of the screen a message says: "Strike a key when ready....."

3. Press: **space bar** The rest of the directory will be displayed and the C> prompt will appear.

Viewing a Wide Directory

To see all of the file names on the screen at once, use the wide directory command. With the C> displayed

1. Type: **dir/w**

2. Press: (ENTER) A display similar to Figure C–6 will appear. Notice that only the file names and extensions are listed in the wide directory format.

Some Things to Remember

Information on a disk is grouped into files. A file is a collection of related information. Each file must have a unique name. File names used in the IBM personal computer environment must follow exact rules.

```
.                    ..              APPEND   EXE   ASSIGN   COM   ATTRIB   EXE
BACKUP   COM   BASIC     COM   BASICA   COM   CHKDSK   COM   COMMAND  COM
COMP     COM   DEBUG     COM   DISKCOMP COM   DISKCOPY COM   EDLIN    COM
FIND     EXE   FORMAT    COM   GRAFTABL COM   GRAPHICS COM   JOIN     EXE
LABEL    COM   MORE      COM   PRINT    COM   RECOVER  COM   REPLACE  EXE
RESTORE  COM   SHARE     EXE   SORT     EXE   SUBST    EXE   TREE     COM
XCOPY    EXE   BASIC     PIF   BASICA   PIF   MORTGAGE BAS   ANSI     SYS
COUNTRY  SYS   DISPLAY   SYS   DRIVER   SYS   FASTOPEN EXE   FDISK    COM
KEYB     COM   KEYBOARD  SYS   MODE     COM   NLSFUNC  EXE   PRINTER  SYS
SELECT   COM   VDISK     SYS   EGA      CPI   LCD      CPI
4201     CPI   5202      CPI   NETBIOS  COM   ANET3    COM
     54 File(s)   27602944 bytes free
```

Figure C-6

- Files names can be 1 to 8 characters long with no embedded spaces.
- The characters can be
  - letters of the alphabet
  - numbers 0 through 9
  - special characters $ # & ! % ( ) - @ _
- File names can be followed by an extension, which is separated from the file name by a period
- Extensions can be one, two or three characters
  - Extensions usually denote the type of file
  - Common extensions are:

.COM	Command
.BAK	Backup copy
.SYS	System
.WPS	Microsoft Works Word Processing
.WKS	*Microsoft Works* Spreadsheet
.WDB	*Microsoft Works* Database

More DOS Activities

In order to complete this section you will need the data disk that came with this book. The C> prompt should be showing on your screen.

Changing Active Drives

As stated earlier, the C> prompt means that DOS is in control of the computer and that any activity you direct DOS to perform will affect disk Drive C:, which is the way DOS refers to the hard disk on this computer. In the instructions that follow, you will learn how to redirect DOS to the floppy disk Drive A and perform activities affecting the contents of that drive.

First, you will examine the contents of the directory of your data disk which will be located in Drive A (note that the colon that appears after the drive letter is part of the drive name and must be included when you type the drive name). With the C> displayed,

1. **Remove any disk that is currently in Drive A** and put it away in its protective envelope.

2. **Insert your data disk into Drive A** and close the drive door.

3. Type: **a:** (remember the colon!).

4. Press: (ENTER) The A> prompt will appear.

5. Type: **dir**

6. Press: (ENTER)   A directory of files and the dates they were created should appear on your screen. Look at the file extensions and see if you can identify the extensions for wordprocessing files, spreadsheet files and database files.

Copying a Single File

By following the steps given below, you will return to Drive C, examine a wide directory of that drive, copy the file *MORE.COM* from the hard disk Drive C to your disk in Drive A and then examine the directory of Drive A to verify that the copy actually occurred. With the A> displayed,

1. Type: c: (need not be in caps).

2. Press: (ENTER)   The C> prompt will reappear.

3. Type: **dir/w**   The wide directory you saw previously will reappear.

4. **Examine the directory to find** *MORE.COM*. If you cannot find that file, ask your instructor for help.

5. Type: **copy more.com a:**   This command tells DOS to copy the file named *MORE.COM* from Drive C and put it on the disk in Drive A using the same file name.

6. **Watch carefully and you will see the red light come on at Drive A as the file is being copied.** When the copy is finished, a message will appear on the screen saying "1 File(s) copied", and the C> prompt will reappear.

7. Type: **dir a:**   This command directs DOS to display a directory of the disk that is currently occupying Drive A. The default active drive still remains C, but for the duration of this one command, DOS will direct its attention to Drive A.

8. Press: (ENTER)   The directory for Drive A will be displayed on the screen.

9. **Look for the file MORE.COM   If you do not see the file name, go back to step 1 and try again.**

Copying a Group of Files

When you want to copy a group of files with similar names you should use the *wild card copy command.* The wild card character (*) can represent any character or group of characters in a file name or file name extension. For example, if you wanted to copy all of the DOS files with the extension ".*EXE*" from Drive C to Drive A, you would use the file name *.EXE* to denote all the files that end in the extension ".EXE". With the C> displayed,

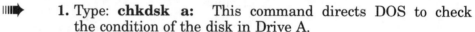 1. Type: **copy *.exe a:**

2. Press: (ENTER) A list of files will appear on the screen as they are being copied. When the copy is finished, a message will appear telling how many files were copied.

3. Type: **dir a:**

4. Press: (ENTER) A directory of all the files on Drive A will appear. Look for the ".EXE" files you just copied.

The Check Disk Command

The *chkdsk* command checks the condition of a disk and reports on the amount of storage space that remains on the disk, the number of files on the disk and any abnormalities that may exist on the disk. With the C> displayed,

1. Type: **chkdsk a:** This command directs DOS to check the condition of the disk in Drive A.

2. Press: (ENTER) A report similar to Figure C–7 will appear.

```
C:\DOS>chkdsk a:

    362496 bytes total disk space
     49152 bytes in 20 user files
    313344 bytes available on disk

    655360 bytes total memory
    397520 bytes free
```

Figure C-7

Printing from the Screen

In computer jargon, the term *hard copy* means to print on paper. There may be times when you will want to get a hard copy of what is currently being displayed on the computer's screen. On the IBM keyboard there is a special key that is used for that purpose. The following instructions will guide you through obtaining a hard copy of the current contents of your screen.

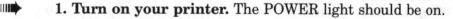 1. **Turn on your printer.** The POWER light should be on.

2. **Press the ON LINE** button if the light is not already on.

3. **If you are using a PC model,** hold down the (SHIFT) key and keep it down while you press the [PRTSC] key. **Release both keys. If you are using an XT model,** you only need to press the [PRTSC] key. The printer should respond almost immediately. If it does not, ask for help.

Disk Operating System (DOS)

DOS is a set of programs that has been revised may times. Each version has a specific number, for example, 1.2 or 3.1. The number after the decimal notes minor changes. The number before the decimal reflects major changes in the software. DOS version 2.0 allowed fixed disks to be used. Version 3.0 made networking possible. Most application software written for the IBM PC will specify the version of DOS which is required. Almost always, a higher version can be substituted for a lower version number. That feature is called *upwards compatibility*. If you don't know the version resident in your computer, here is a DOS command to check the version of DOS you have on your disk. With the C> displayed,

  1. Type: **ver**

2. Press: (ENTER)   The message shown in Figure C–8 will appear (version number may differ).

```
C:\DOS>ver

IBM Personal Computer DOS Version  3.30
```

Figure C-8

Cleaning Up Your Data Disk

You will now remove from your data disk the files you just copied since they are no longer needed. With the C> displayed,

1. Type: **erase a:more.com**   You will be deleting the file *MORE.COM* from your data disk in Drive A.

2. Press: (ENTER)

3. Type: **erase a:*.exe**   All files with the extension ".EXE" will be deleted from your data disk in Drive A.

4. Press: (ENTER)

5. **Remove your disk from Drive A.**

6. **Turn the computer off.**

Some More Things to Remember

DOS programs help you operate the computer but you need application programs to do specific tasks. The DOS system contains programs that manage the disk drives, the memory and peripherals.

Application programs like word processors and spreadsheets help you to perform a particular task. DOS must be loaded into the computer before loading the application program.

Application programs with DOS have both DOS and applications on the same disk. DOS can be "installed" on any application disk. If DOS is not on the disk, you will get the message: "Non-system disk or disk error" if you attempt to start the computer with that disk.

Data disks hold your files. Data disks are used with application programs.

Summary

As you worked through the exercises in this Appendix you have practiced some powerful DOS commands, but more important, we hope you learned some of the reasons why an operating system such as DOS is needed. You can learn more about the operating system from the DOS manual that came with your computer.

Installing *Microsoft Works* on a Hard Disk

If you have not installed DOS on to your hard disk, do so before continuing with this worksheet. Consult your computer manual for assistance.

Before installing *Works,* find out with which video card your computer is equipped. Your *Works* manual describes the installation procedure; however, here is a brief summary of the process.

⯈ **1. Turn on your computer.** After the drive lights go off,

2. **Insert the Setup/Utilities** disk that came with your *Works* package in Drive A. When the C> appears

3. Type: **a:setup**

4. Press: (ENTER) A welcome message will appear.

5. **Follow the directions on the screen** to complete the installation procedure.

Use the ⊕ to select the proper option when requested. If the desired option is already highlighted, simply press (ENTER).

During the setup procedure to install *Works* on the hard disk, you will be asked for a directory name for the *Works* program, your type of video card, and the printer port you are using. Answer these questions as they appear. The instructions in the body of this book assume that you have installed *Works* in a directory named WORKS. If you have limited space on your hard disk, you need not copy the chart fonts, *Learning Microsoft Works* (tutorial), mouse, or Ms-Key. If you are given the option of high or low resolution for your printer, choose low to avoid time-consuming printouts.

6. Press: (ENTER) when you see the message **Leave SETUP.**

You are now ready to use the *Works* program.

E Using *Microsoft Works* with Two Floppy Drives

If you have a two-floppy disk system rather than a hard disk, follow the instructions below to "boot" the system with the DOS disk and load the *Works* program.

1. **Insert your DOS disk (2.0 or higher) in Drive A.**

2. **Turn on your computer.**

3. **Type the date and time or, if you prefer, press** (ENTER) **twice** to skip the date and time prompts.

4. **When the A> appears, remove the DOS disk.**

5. **Insert the *Works* Program disk in Drive A.**

6. **Insert your data disk in Drive B.**

7. Type: **works** (need not be in caps).

After the copyright information appears, the NEW menu will appear. (See Figure E–1.)

If you choose the OPEN option, the next screen will show the OPEN dialog box with the files on the disk in Drive A listed. Since you need a list of the files on the data disk which is in Drive B,

8. Press: (TAB) to move the highlight to the "Other Drives & Directories" box.

9. Press: (↓) to highlight **B.**

10. Press: (ENTER) The files on your data disk should now be listed in the extreme left-hand box.

You can now proceed with instructions in the individual worksheets.

Figure E-1

F Establishing the CompuServe Connection

Getting Started

This appendix assumes that your computer is properly equipped with a Hayes compatible modem, that the cabling and phone lines are connected, and that *Microsoft Works* is properly installed on your computer's hard disk.

Establishing a CompuServe account includes three distinct operations. First you must purchase the CompuServe starter pack from a software vendor. Second, you initiate a temporary account, using information from the starter pack. Finally, CompuServe will mail you your permanent account information.

There are a few questions you must answer and a file you must prepare before you can **log on** (connect your computer) to CompuServe's computers for the first time. The next section will explain those questions.

Preparing a Sign-up Worksheet

Record your answers to these questions on the worksheet which follows.

Question 1: Which phone number will you use to call the service?

You can connect directly to CompuServe by using one of the numbers listed in the starter pack, or you can get the closest number from their toll free customer service department. CompuServe's connect time charges are the same for day and night.

If a local CompuServe number is not available, other phone carriers like Tymnet or Telenet supply lines for an additional surcharge.

Select the phone number you plan to use and write it on the worksheet. Remember to include any extra numbers you may need to get an outside line. You must insert commas in the phone number to create a pause in the dialing sequence that is sometimes needed to get an outside line. Each comma results in a two-second pause with Hayes compatible modems.

If you have the call-waiting feature on your phone, an incoming call may cause your modem to become disconnected. Your local telephone company should be able to tell you how to temporarily disable the call-waiting feature when using your modem.

Question 2: What information will CompuServe require?

Your temporary ID number, password, agreement number and serial number are found in your starter pack. CompuServe passwords should consist of two unrelated words and must include at least one non-alphanumeric character (+, ¢, %, etc.).

Question 3: How will you pay for services?

There are three payment options. The first is Master Charge or VISA. If you use this method, write the requested information on the worksheet. The second method is "check free" which transfers the amount due every month electronically from your checking account. For this option fill in the blanks on the worksheet under "check free." The last option is Business Account Billing and requires prior approval from CompuServe. For a more complete explanation of the options, see your starter pack.

Question 4: What type of equipment do you have?

To display information on your screen, the host computer must know the number of characters which can be displayed on one line. Most monitors display 80 characters per line. You must also know how many lines of text can be displayed at one time. Usually 25 lines fit on the screen unless your communications program itself uses some lines at the top or bottom of the screen. CompuServe has help screeens during the sign on process which will tell you the number of characters and lines your screen will display.

Question 5: Do you want the executive option?

Additional services and data bases are available for an added cost; you will not be using this option for this exercise. You can read about it in the CompuServe booklet in the starter pack.

Setting up the Works Communications File

While you are off line (or not connected), you will enter information into the *Works* communications file so that the computer can transmit that information as quickly as possible when you do go on line. *Remember:* The more you can do off line the better because you pay for connect time by the minute.

To enter the phone number,

1. **Insert your data disk into Drive A and close the drive door.**

2. Press: (ALT) to activate the Menu bar.

SIGN-UP WORKSHEET

1. CompuServe Phone #: _____

2. User data:
User ID# _____

Password _____

Agreement # _____

Serial # _____

3. Payment Option: Credit Card

Credit Card Number _____

Type (MC or VISA) _____

Issued by which bank? _____

Expiration date _____

If Master Charge, interbank number _____

Payment option: "Check free"

Routing transit number _____
                             (9 digits in lower left corner of check)

Checking account number _____

Number of next check in checkbook _____

Bank's name _____
Bank's address _____

Payment option: Business Account
Requires prior approval of CompuServe.

4. Computer information:

Number of characters on one line _____

Number of lines of text on one screen _____

5. Executive option: _____

3. Type: **O** to select the OPTIONS menu. The OPTIONS menu allows you to change the communications settings.

4. Type: **P**   (The PHONE dialog box will appear.)

5. **Type the phone number you will use.**

6. Press: (TAB) until the cursor is in the Dial Type box. Leave Tone selected if you have a touch tone phone. If you have a dial phone, use the (→) to move the selection to Pulse.

7. Press: (TAB) until <OK> is selected.

8. Press: (ENTER) to complete entering the number.

Setting the Communications Settings ▐▐▐➡

To record the communications settings (parameters),

1. Press: (ALT)

2. Press: **O** to select the OPTIONS menu.

3. Press: **C** to select the COMMUNICATIONS option. The COMMUNICATIONS dialog box will appear and you can enter the settings of the computer with which you wish to communicate. Remember that the two computers must have the same settings to be able to communicate. You will use the following settings for CompuServe:

    Baud Rate: 300
    Data Bits: 7
    Stop Bits: 1
    Handshake: Xon/Xoff
    Parity: Even
    Port: COM1

4. Type: **300**   This is the least expensive rate and the one you should use while learning. Later on you may wish to move up to 1200 baud if your modem can handle that rate.

5. Press: (TAB) to move the cursor to the Data Bits box.

6. Press: (←) to select 7 bits.

7. Press: (TAB) to move the cursor to the Stop Bit box. The setting should be 1.

8. Press: (TAB) to move the cursor to the Parity Box.

9. Press: (↑) until EVEN is selected.

10. Press: (TAB) to move the cursor to the Handshake box. Xon/Xoff should be selected.

11. Press: (TAB) to move the cursor to the Port box. COM1 should be selected to send serial data through communications line 1.

12. Press: (TAB) to move the cursor to <OK>.

13. Press: (ENTER) to complete setting the parameters.

Saving the Settings

You should save the parameter settings so you will not have to reenter the information each time you want to log on to CompuServe. Your data disk should be in Drive A.

1. Press: (ALT)

2. Type: **F** to select the FILE menu.

3. Type: **A** to select the SAVE AS option.

4. Type: **COMPUS.WCM** This file name will cause the parameter settings to be saved in a file named *COMPUS.WCM*.

5. Press: (TAB)

6. Press: (↓) twice to select Drive A.

7. Press: (TAB) to select <OK>.

8. Press: (ENTER) to save the file.

By creating a separate file for each service or person you call, the computer can recall and automatically dial the appropriate phone number when prompted.

Connecting to CompuServe

You are now ready to call CompuServe.

1. Press: (ALT)

2. Type: **C** to select the CONNECT menu.

3. Press: (ENTER) to select the CONNECT option. The Status bar at the bottom of the screen should tell you that the modem is dialing. If the connection is successful, the Status bar will change from OFFLINE to an elapsed time indicator. The word "CONNECT" will appear on the screen. If the connection is unsuccessful, the words "NO CARRIER" will appear on the screen. Try again by starting over from step 1 above. When you have a successful connection,

4. Press: (CTRL)-**C** You will be asked for your user ID number.

5. **Type your ID number from the worksheet.**

6. Press: (ENTER) You will be asked for the password.

7. **Type the password from the worksheet.** To help protect the privacy of your password, the letters you type will not appear on the screen.

8. Press: (ENTER)   If the message "invalid entry" appears, press (CTRL)-C together to obtain the prompt and type the password again. Eventually, a message should appear asking for your Agreement number.

9. **Type the Agreement number from your worksheet.** You will be asked for the serial number.

10. **Type the serial number from your worksheet.** A welcome message should appear together with information about the amount of credit time you have available. After that, the service terms and conditions will be displayed on the screen. (They are also given in the starter pack.)

11. Type: **agree** (lower or upper case is OK).

12. Press: (ENTER)   After a description of the CompuServe service, you will be asked if you want the Executive option.

13. Type: **no**

14. Press: (ENTER)

15. **Type your name, mailing address and phone numbers** when you are prompted to do so. Your permanent password and magazine will be sent to the address you enter. Now for the money issue. How will you pay for extra charges?

16. **Type the information from your worksheet about your charge account or checking account** when you are prompted to do so. You have not yet been charged for the connect time but you will be for future sessions.

17. CompuServe will now give you a permanent ID number and temporary password. **Write these down** and place them in a safe place. If anyone uses these numbers, the charges will be made to your account. The charges begin the next time you log on with your permanent ID.

Equipment Questions

18. **Respond to the questions about your equipment when they appear on the screen.** CompuServe needs to know about your system so that it can send data in the correct format. Up to now, you have seen 32 characters across the screen. CompuServe doesn't know about the size of your screen and will adjust the line length when appropriate. If you are not sure of the size of the screen, respond YES when CompuServe asks if you need help. Numbers will be

placed on the screen, and you will be able to tell the exact numbers of lines and characters your screen can display.

19. **Select #6 (Other General Purpose) in response to the question about your terminal type** unless you know exactly what type of terminal you have.

20. **Enter the other data about your screen from your worksheet in response to the appropriate prompts from CompuServe.**

You will now be given a chance to change the settings, and you will get a listing of the CompuServe commands. These commands are listed in your starter pack. When you are satisfied with the settings,

21. Press: (CTRL)-O to break out of the display.

22. Press: (ENTER)

Quitting CompuServe

It is always a good idea to log off of a service before disconnecting. Most information services charge by the minute, and you may be charged for the time it takes for the service to determine that you have hung up.

To disconnect from CompuServe,

 1. Type: **bye**

2. Press: (ENTER)

Disconnecting *Works*

To disconnect the COMMUNICATIONS option, you must repeat the same steps you used to connect.

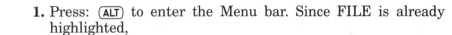 1. Press: (ALT)

2. Type: **C** to select the CONNECT menu.

3. Press: (ENTER) to select the CONNECT option. The OK TO DISCONNECT dialog box will appear.

4. Press: (ENTER) to disconnect.

Quitting *Works*

1. Press: (ALT) to enter the Menu bar. Since FILE is already highlighted,

2. Press: (ENTER)

3. Type: **x** to select the exit option.

4. **Take your disk out of Drive A and place it in the protective envelope.**

5. **Turn the computer off.**

G Quick Menu Reference Sheets

Wordprocessing

Note: These menu reference sheets will help you see what options are available in the basic Menu bars, even those not used in these worksheets. To see submenu items, refer to the *Microsoft Works Reference* manual. Some commands are toggle switches. When you use a toggle key for the first time, it turns the activity on; when you press it again, it turns off the activity.

OPTION	FUNCTION
FILE menu	
New	Opens a new file (document)
Open	Displays an Open dialog box with which you open an existing file
Save	Saves a document
Save **A**s	Saves a document under a new name
Sav**e All**	Saves all open files
DOS	Enters the Disk Operating System without leaving *Works*
E**x**it	Leaves *Works* and returns to DOS
EDIT menu	
Undo	Ignores last command; restores document to previous state
Move	Moves selected copy from one location to another
Copy	Copies selected copy to another part of the document
Copy Special	Copies format of selected copy to another section of document
Delete	Deletes selected text

Insert Special	Inserts wide variety of special characters such as end-of-line mark and optional hyphen
Insert Field	Inserts placeholders where database information will be printed
Insert Chart	Inserts placeholder where specified chart will be printed

PRINT menu

Print	Prints document to a printer or to disk
Layout	Lets you specify margins, paper sizes, footers, headers
Print Merge	Prints form letters and other similar documents
Print Labels	Prints mailing labels using a database file
Select Text Printer	Selects printer to be used

SELECT menu

Go To	Displays page you specify
Search	Searches for text you specify
Replace	Searches for text and replaces with new text

FORMAT menu

Plain Text	Returns text to normal display
Bold	Darkens the selected text on screen and when printed
Underline	Underlines selected text when printed
Italic	Prints selected text in italics
Character	Indicates character formats such as bold, italics, underline, super/subscript, strikethrough, and print size
Normal Paragraph	Changes format of selected paragraph to default setting: left-aligned, single-spaced, no spaces before or after
Left	Aligns text at left margin

Center	Aligns text at the center of the line	
Justified	Aligns text at the right margin	
Single Space	Leaves no blank lines between text lines	
Double Space	Leaves one blank line between selected lines	
Paragraph	Displays indents, alignment, line spacing for paragraphs	
Tabs	Enables you to reset tabs	

OPTIONS menu

Split	Enables you to display two parts of the document at one time; this is a toggle switch.
Show Ruler	Toggle to display or hide ruler at the top of the screen
Show All Characters	Displays paragraph, tab, and spacing symbols; this is a toggle switch.
Headers and Footers	Displays header and footer lines at the top of the screen; this is a toggle switch.
Check Spelling	Searches for misspelled words and lets you correct them
Manual Pagination	Activates/deactivates manual pagination
Paginate Now	Repaginates file if manual pagination is on

WINDOW

Help Index	Reviews *Works* features
Tutorial Index	Allows you to practice sample lessons
Settings	Allows you to change various default settings

Spreadsheet

FILE menu	(See Word Processing menu reference)
EDIT menu	
Move	Moves contents of the selected cell(s), leaving the selected cells empty
Copy	Copies selected cell(s) to another part of the spreadsheet or to other *Works* files

Copy **S**pecial	Allows you to add or subtract selected cells from other cells, copy values only, or convert formulas to values
Cl**e**ar	Erases content of selected cells; formats are unaffected
Delete	Removes selected columns or rows; entire rows or columns must be selected
Insert	Adds entire columns or rows between existing columns or rows; entire rows or columns must be selected
Fill **R**ight	Copies the extreme left-hand column of selected cells into the selected cells immediately to the right
Fill Down	Copies the top row of selected cell(s) to selected cells below
Name	Creates and deletes names for cells and ranges

PRINT menu

Print	Prints selected spreadsheet on the printer or a disk
Layout	Lets you set margins, paper sizes, footnotes, headers
Set Print **A**rea	Allows you to print a portion of your worksheet
Insert Page Break	Inserts a page break above or to the left of the selected row or column; entire row/column must be selected
Delete Page Break	Removes manual page breaks
Font	Selects the font (type face) and font size
Print **C**hart	Used to print charts using selected spreadsheet data
Se**l**ect Text Printer	Selects printer to be used

SELECT menu

Row	Expands the current selection to entire row(s)

Column	Expands the current selection to entire column(s)
Go To	Moves highlight to cell or range you specify
Search	Searches cells for a series of specified characters; (F7) continues the search

FORMAT menu

General	Formats as precisely as possible within cell limits
Fixed	Sets number of decimals displayed in selected cells(s) according to your specifications
Dollar	Inserts dollar sign and commas every three places
Comma	Inserts commas every three places
Percent	Multiplies by 100 and inserts percent sign
Exponential	Displays selected cells in scientific notation
Logical	Displays TRUE or FALSE in place of a numeric value
Time/Date	Converts numerical values to a date or time
Style	Aligns, styles (bold, underline, italic), and locks or unlocks selected cells
Width	Changes width of selected column

OPTIONS menu

Freeze **T**itles	Specifies rows and/or columns containing headings which should NOT scroll
Unfreeze Titles	Reverses the above command
Split	Permits division of work area into two or four smaller work areas and back again by using the down and right arrows
Show **F**ormulas	Displays and hides the formulas rather than values on the spreadsheet; this is a toggle switch
Protect	Enables and disables protection of cell contents

Manual Calculations	Turns automatic calculation on and off
Calculate Now	Immediately calculates all of the formulas

CHART menu

Define	Displays chart screen and vice versa if the computer has a graphics card
New	Creates new chart
View	Displays the active chart
Charts	Copies, deletes, renames charts

WINDOW menu (See Word Processing menu reference)

Database

OPTION	FUNCTION	VIEW
FILE menu	(See Word Processing menu reference)	
EDIT menu		
Move	Moves entire record(s) or field(s) within the database	List, Form, Design
Copy	In List view, copies selected cell(s) to another part of the database. In Form view, copies the entire record.	List, Form
Clear	Erases content of selected fields; no effect on cells containing formulas	List, Form, Query
Delete	Removes selected record(s) or field(s) from database	List, Form, Design, Query
Insert	Adds record(s) or field(s); entire record or field must be selected for insert to work in List view	List, Form
Fill Right	Copies extreme left-hand column of selected cells into the selected cells to the right	List
Fill Down	Copies top row of selected cells into selected cells below	List

Name	Names or renames selected field	List

PRINT menu

Print	Sends selected data to a printer or to disk	List
Layout	Lets you specify margins, paper sizes, footers, headers for a report	List, Form
Insert Page Break	Inserts page breaks above or to the left of selected record or field; entire record or field must be selected	List
Delete Page Break	Removes manually set page breaks	List
Font	Selects font (type faces) and font size for printed reports	List, Form
Print Report	Prints active report	List, Form
Select Text Printer	Selects printer to be used	List, Form

SELECT menu

Record	Expands current selection to include entire record	List
Field	Expands current selection to include entire field	List
Go To	Selects record and field you specify	List, Form
Search	Searches for characters you specify; (F7) continues the search	List, Form

FORMAT menu	(See Spreadsheet menu reference)	

OPTIONS menu

Split	Enables splitting the screen to display two or four windows; also reverses the action	List

Define Form	Displays Design form on which you can create, change, and rearrange fields and fieldnames	Form
Protect	Enables and disables protection of database	List, Form
View Form	Displays records in database as individual forms	List
View List	Displays records in a list, one record per line	Form

QUERY menu

Define	Use to create or change query (question)	List, Form
Apply **Q**uery	Carries out query command on all records	List, Form
Hide Record	Suppresses display of selected records	List, Form
Show **A**ll Records	Displays all records, including hidden ones	List, Form
Switch Hidden Records	Displays hidden records and hides others	List, Form
Sort	Arranges all records in either ascending or descending order based on one to three fields	List, Form

REPORT menu

Define	Displays blank report screen for creating new report	List, Form
New	Creates a new report using Speed Reporting	List, Form
View	Displays the active report	List, Form
Save **A**s	Displays dialog box for saving the report	List, Form
Reports	Copies, names, or deletes reports	List, Form
WINDOW	(See Word Processing menu reference)	

Glossary

ABSOLUTE CELL REFERENCE. In the spreadsheet application, a reference to a cell location in a worksheet that remains unchanged if a formula that contains the reference is moved to a new location. *See* RELATIVE REFERENCE.

ANALOG SIGNALS. Electrical signals which change continuously in wave form, such as the human voice. The telephone is an analog device since it turns voice vibrations into analogous electrical vibrations. *See* DIGITAL SIGNALS.

APPLICATION SOFTWARE. Computer programs that apply the resources and capabilities of the computer and its peripheral devices to a task, such as word processing, database management, graphics or communications. *Compare* SYSTEM SOFTWARE definition.

ASCII CODE. Acronym for American Standard Code for Information Interchange. Used in almost all personal computer data communications.

AUXILIARY MEMORY. The component of a computer used to permanently store programs and data. Disks and tapes are used for auxiliary memory. Programs and data must be read into the computer's main memory before they can be processed.

BACKUP. As a verb, to make a duplicate copy of a file or program on a disk in case the original is lost or destroyed. As a noun, the duplicate copy itself is often referred to as the "back-up."

BASIC. Beginner's All-purpose Symbolic Instruction Code. A computer language developed at Dartmouth College during the late 60s and early 70s. BASIC is available in most personal computers and is relatively easy for programming novices to learn.

BAUD RATE. A unit for measuring the speed of data transmission.

BIT. Binary Digit. The smallest unit of data stored in a computer. The value of an individual bit is represented by the number 1 (on) or the number O (off).

BOOT. The process of starting up a computer by loading a program into RAM memory from a disk. *See* WARM BOOT.

BUFFER. A group of storage locations within which data are stored while waiting to be transferred between the computer and a peripheral device.

BULLETIN BOARD. A program stored on a host computer which allows messages to be posted and read via modem for other computer users.

BYTE. A set of eight bits grouped together to form a storage location in the computer main memory. A computer's memory is usually described in terms of BYTES. One BYTE can store one typed character. In some computers, each byte is individually addressable. In other computers, sets of bytes are grouped together to form an addressable computer word.

CELL. Intersection of a row and column in a spreadsheet.

CGA. Color Graphics Adapter. IBM's first product to display color and graphics. Allows display of four out of 16 simultaneous colors. *See* EGA.

CHIPS. Integrated circuits made by photographically etching electronic circuits onto a tiny wafer of silicon no larger than a fraction of an inch on each side.

COLD BOOT. Starting the computer when the power is off. *See* BOOT.

COMMAND. An order for the computer to execute some specific task, usually immediately. Some common commands are SAVE, RUN, or LOAD.

COMMUNICATIONS. The capability of a computer to send information to and receive information from another computer.

COMPUTER. An electronic device that performs predefined and internally stored (programmed) computations at high speed and with great accuracy.

COMPUTER LANGUAGE. A code for giving the computer instructions. Some common computer languages are: BASIC, Pascal, FORTRAN, and COBOL. A set of instructions written in a computer language is called a program. Computer languages are also called programming languages.

COM PORTS. *See* SERIAL PORTS.

CONTROL KEY. A special key on the computer's keyboard that is used in conjunction with other keys to change their normal meaning. The CONTROL KEY usually must be held down while another key is depressed.

CPU. The Central Processing Unit, also called the microprocessor in personal computers. The part of the computer that directs the flow of information within the computer, performs all calculations, and controls all other components of the computer.

CRT. Cathode Ray Tube in a video display unit (VDT). Computer jargon for the display screen connected to a computer.

CURSOR. A marker displayed on the computer monitor which usually designates where the next typed character will be displayed.

DATABASE. A collection of data or information concerning one major topic maintained in one central storage place or file, for example, the telephone book or card catalog at a library.

DATA DISK. A disk used for storing documents created or used by the user, such as letters, memos, graphs, etc. Compare with PROGRAM DISK definition.

DECIMAL TAB STOP. Automatically lines up the decimal points in a column of numbers.

DEFAULT. The standard setting or action performed by the software when no specific direction is given to the computer by the user.

DEVICE. A unit of computer hardware, such as a disk drive or printer. Sometimes called a peripheral or peripheral device.

DIALOG BOX. Windows which display different options at given points in a program.

DIGITAL SIGNALS. Unlike ANALOG signals, digital signals can have only two levels (binary) and nothing in between. All standard microcomputers use digital logic. Additional components must be added to intercept signals for transmission and reception of analog signals.

DIRECTORY. An index file containing the names of all the files contained on a storage medium.

DISK. A flat, circular piece of plastic (flexible) or metal (rigid) onto which information is recorded magnetically. A flexible disk is also called a "floppy." The 3 1/4" floppy disk encased in a rigid container is sometimes called a "micro-floppy."

DISK DRIVE. A device that can read information from and write information onto a disk in much the same way that a tape recorder plays from or records on to magnetic tape. Inside the drive, a motor spins the disk and a read/write head performs the reading or writing operation.

DISK OPERATING SYSTEM (DOS). An operating system which allows a computer to use disks for data storage. Many computer manufacturers incorporate the acronym, DOS, into the name of the operating system for a particular computer: for example, IBM PC/DOS or MS/DOS for IBM personal computers. On many personal computers, the operating system is loaded into RAM when the computer is booted with a System Master disk. Some personal computers may have an operating system resident in ROM. *See* OPERATING SYSTEM.

DISPLAY. As a noun, the screen connected to the computer; see CRT or MONITOR. As a verb, to cause material to appear on the computer screen.

DOCUMENTATION. Written instructions that describe how to use computer hardware or software.

DOWNLOAD. To save a program or file sent to your computer by another computer, as opposed to letting it disappear as it scrolls off the screen.

DUPLEX. "Full Duplex" — data transmission in both directions at the same time; "half duplex" — transmission in one direction only.

EGA. Enhanced Graphics Adapter. Enables monitor to display higher graphics and text resolutions. Able to display 16 out of a possible 64 simultaneous colors. An upgrade from CGA, it is the current standard for graphics and text applications on IBM and compatible computers.

ESCAPE key. Standard control key available on most computer keyboards. May be used to take control of the computer away from a program, to escape from a specific program, or to stop a program. In *Works,* it usually moves the program back to the previous step.

EXTENSION. Term referring to the part of the file name after the period to describe or further identify the contents of that file.

FIELD. Smallest unit of a database record.

FILE. A unit of information that is stored on disk and given a file name. The contents of a file may be anything—a letter, a financial model, a graph, or a program.

FIRMWARE. A computer program or set of programs stored in the computer's ROM memory. Firmware is not lost when the computer is turned off.

FLOPPY DISK. *See* DISK.

FONT. In *Works* terminology, the typeface or design used to print characters, for example, Courier or Helvetica. *Works* also lists pica and elite as fonts. In typesetting terminology, font is used to describe the combination of typeface and typestyle used to print characters, for example, Courier/bold.

FORM FEED. The manual control that causes the printer to advance the paper to the top of the next page for continuous feed paper; if single sheets are being used, the current sheet will be ejected.

FORMAT. (1) As a verb, to prepare the surface of a floppy disk so it can be used for storing data. (2) As a noun, the pattern which must be written on the disk before it can be used for storing data. Different computers require different disk formats. Also used both as a noun and a verb to describe the manner in which text is set up on a page.

FORMULA. A rule expressed as an equation.

FUNCTION KEYS. Special keys which when depressed will begin some activity as prescribed by the software.

HARD COPY. The printed material generated by a computer. Also called printouts.

HARD DISK. Fast auxiliary storage mounted in its own case or inside a computer. Capable of storing millions of characters—typically 10M, 20M, or 40M. *See* WINCHESTER DRIVE.

HARDWARE. The physical components of a computer system.

HAYES MODEM. The standard communication device used by the majority of communication programs. Hayes compatible means that a communication device will operate much like the Hayes modem.

HIGH-LEVEL LANGUAGE. A computer programming language that employs English-like words and statements rather than numeric codes.

INITIALIZE. *See* definition (1) under FORMAT.

INSTRUCTION. One statement in a computer program.

INTEGRATED PROGRAM. Software that combines two or more types of applications software. *Works* is an integrated program which combines word processing, database, spreadsheet, and communication applications. Data can be easily exchanged between them.

INTERACTIVE PROGRAM. A program that allows the computer and the user to respond to each other.

INTERFACE. A hardware device or a computer program that allows one component of the computer to communicate with another. Interfaces are commonly used between the computer and a printer or between the computer and a modem.

JUSTIFICATION. Pertaining to alignment of text in the center or at the left margin, right margin, or both. *Works* calls this alignment.

KEYBOARD. A device used by the user to enter information into the RAM memory of the computer.

KILOBYTE. A measure of memory size, often abbreviated as K. One kilobyte (1K) is 1,024 characters or bytes. *See* MEGABYTE.

LPT PORTS. *See* PARALLEL PORTS.

LABEL. Non-numeric entries in a spreadsheet. Calculations cannot be performed on cells containing labels.

LAYOUT. The physical placement of text or data on the printed page.

LINE FEED. The manual control that advances the paper one line at a time.

LOAD. A common command which tells a computer to transfer a program or data file from a disk or tape into its main memory.

LOG OFF. *Also Logoff*. To break an established connection with a computer that serves more than one user. The Log Off procedure will vary from system to system. Some typical Log Off commands are "Exit", "Logoff", "LO", and "Bye".

LOG ON. *Also Logon*. To gain access to a computer that serves more than one user. The Log On procedure will vary from system to system, but usually requires that the computer be supplied with a predetermined account name and unique password for each individual user.

MAINFRAME. A large computer in contrast to a minicomputer or a microcomputer (personal computer) in terms of physical size, size of memory, and speed of calculations.

MAIN MEMORY. The component of a computer used to temporarily store programs and data for quick access by the CPU. Personal computers use RAM chips for main memory.

MEGABYTE. One million bytes, or one million characters. Commonly abbreviated as M. *See* KILOBYTE.

MENU. A visual display on the computer's monitor that lists the activities the computer can perform. The user selects the desired activity by moving the cursor to it, or by typing a letter or number associated with the desired activity.

MICROPROCESSOR. The most important chip in the computer. It executes instructions from programs and controls all the components of the system.

MODEM. A peripheral device that enables one computer to communicate directly with another computer by using telephone communications channels. MODEM is an acronym for MOdulator/DEModulator. A MODEM changes the digital electronic signals used by a computer into analog wave forms that can be transmitted by telephone and vice versa.

MONITOR. A video display connected to the computer and used as an output device. *See* CRT.

MONOCHROME. Single color display.

MOTHERBOARD. Main circuit board of a microcomputer.

OFFLINE. In the communications application, this means that the computers are not electronically connected.

ONLINE. In the communications application, this means that the computer is now electronically connected to another computer.

ON LINE LIGHT. The indicator that shows that the printer is ready to print and receive commands from the computer. When the light is off the printer will respond to manual controls only.

OPERATING SYSTEM. A collection of system software which controls the internal operations of the computer and provides certain utility functions to the user. Different operating systems are designed for different computers.

PARALLEL PORTS. The input/output outlet in which eight bits are transmitted simultaneously instead of one at a time (serially).

PARAMETERS. Settings for communication software which enable computers to send and receive data via modem.

PARITY. In communications, a form of error checking used to increase the chances that each character has been received correctly.

PERIPHERALS. Devices connected to a computer system which are not essential to its operation. Modems and printers are peripherals.

PERSONAL COMPUTER. A microcomputer. *See* MAIN-FRAME.

PLACEHOLDERS. In *Works,* special characters used in wordprocessing documents to set off fields which are to be replaced by database data during printing.

POINT. The unit of measurement for type size.

PRINTER. The hardware that is used to obtain printed copies of data produced by the computer.

PROGRAM. Causes the computer to do something. Programs are also called software.

PROGRAM DISK. A disk containing a program. *Compare with* DATA DISK.

PROMPT. A character or message provided by the computer to indicate that it is ready to accept keyboard input.

QUERY. Question process which allows you to search a database for records which meet selected criteria.

RAM. Random Access Memory. Temporary memory on chips. The main memory of a computer. All programs are loaded into RAM memory before they can be run. RAM memory is called "volatile" or "temporary" because the programs or data stored there are lost when the computer is turned off.

RGB MONITOR. A monitor that creates color from Red, Green, and Blue signals. *See* CGA, EGA.

RELATIVE REFERENCE. In the spreadsheet application, a reference to a cell location in a worksheet that changes if the formula is moved to a new location. *See* ABSOLUTE REFERENCE.

READ. To take data from a disk, tape, or keyboard, and place it into the computer's memory. Reading is an input operation.

RECORD. A collection of related items of information treated as a unit. Description of an entity in a database.

ROM. Read Only Memory. Permanent memory stored on chips which provide fast access. Anything stored in ROM remains there even when the computer is turned off. ROM chips are programmed at the time of manufacture.

RS-232-C. A standard developed by the Electronics Industry Association specifying what signals and voltages will be used to transmit data from a computer to a modem.

RUN. A common command that tells a computer to perform the activities defined in the program currently stored in its memory.

SAVE. A common command that tells a computer to transfer a program or a file from main memory to a disk or tape.

SCREEN. The surface portion of a video terminal on which information is displayed.

SCROLL. Process of viewing a program or file by having it continuously display on the screen from beginning to end.

SERIAL PORT. Also referred to as COM1 or COM2 on an IBM Personal Computer or compatible. Data is transferred one bit at a time through a serial port. Used for modem connections and some printer connections.

SILICON. Basic semiconductor material obtained from sand which is used for the development of chips.

SOFTWARE. Another name for programs. Software may be written by the computer user, it may be purchased for a special purpose, or it may be delivered with the computer.

SPLIT SCREEN. Command that divides the computer screen into two or more windows (work areas). Each window can show a different part of the same file.

SPREADSHEET. A type of program that arranges data and formulas in a matrix of cells.

SYSTEM SOFTWARE. The set of computer programs that make up the operating system. They are usually supplied with the computer and are always computer specific.

TEMPLATE. A frequently-used form stored as a file that can be used whenever the information varies but not the format.

TERMINAL. Input/Output device (keyboard/display or keyboard/printer).

TOGGLE KEY. A key that alternately turns an activity on and off when you press it more than one time.

TYPEFACE. The design of the printed characters, for example, Courier, Helvetica, Times. *See* FONT.

TYPESTYLE. The variation of typeface used, such as bold, italic, underline.

UNDO. A command that will reverse the most recent user action.

UTILITY PROGRAM. Program which performs common tasks or tasks essential to file maintenance, for example, sorting, file recovery, etc.

VGA. Video Graphics Array. Displays higher resolution than EGA.

VALUE. In spreadsheet terminology, numeric entries or formulas. *Contrast with* LABEL.

WARM BOOT. Loading a computer program when the computer is already turned on. On the IBM PC, press (CTRL)-(ALT)-(DEL) simultaneously. *See* BOOT.

WILD CARD. Using a special character to stand for any other character or group of characters. A method of handling multiple files without specifying each file by its full, unique name.

WINCHESTER DISK DRIVE. A set of rigid disks permanently sealed into a disk drive. Provides greater storage capacity and offers less risk of data loss than do floppy disks.

WINDOW. A viewing area of a portion of computer memory as displayed on the video screen. Some programs allow multiple windows to be displayed at the same time, allowing the viewer to see different parts of a file at the same time.

WORDPROCESSING. Technique of electronically storing, editing, and manipulating text by using a computer.

WORDWRAP. In word processing, when a word exceeds the right margin the program will automatically move the word to the next line.

WRITE. To transfer data or programs from the computer's memory to disks, tapes, monitors, or printer. An output operation.

WRITE PROTECT. A procedure to prevent accidental writing to a disk or tape.

X-AXIS. In charting, the horizontal line usually showing the way data is classified, for example, days, months, years, products, etc.

Y-AXIS. In charting, the vertical line that represents the unit of measurement or amount, for example, dollars, number of products sold, etc.

Index